Trucial Oman Scouts on patrol

Photo courtesy of *Soldier* Magazine

Are You the Man?

MEMORIES OF LIFE IN THE TRUCIAL OMAN SCOUTS

Edited by

TERRY WARD

AND

HUGH NICKLIN

From a proposal by Tony Ford

© COPYRIGHT: Trucial Oman Scouts Association 2014The rights of the Trucial Oman Scouts Association to be identified as the creators of this work have been asserted hereto in accordance with the Copyright Designs and Patents Act 1988.All rights reserved.Book design and layout created on a Mac by Hugh Nicklin.Dust jacket design by Terry Ward.Photographs are from the Trucial Oman Scouts Archive unless otherwise stated.This book is sold subject to the condition that it shall not, by way of trade, be lent, re-sold, hired out, or otherwise circulated or adapted without the aforesaid Association's prior consent.

DEDICATION

*In memory of all those Trucial Oman Scouts
no longer with us*

Find out more at
www.trucialomanscouts.org

CONTENTS

Contents		Page
Foreward		vi
Preface		vii
Maps of the region		xiv
Chapter 1	Mutiny at Buraimi Oasis	15
Chapter 2	Codes, Roads and Rebels	25
Chapter 3	The Five-Year Man	44
Chapter 4	Model T Ford in the TOS	54
Chapter 5	Itchy Feet Can Take You Places	62
Chapter 6	A Cook's Tour	75
Chapter 7	Banished from Sharjah	89
Chapter 8	Training the Abu Dhabi Defence Force	100
Chapter 9	Sparks Across Arabia	107
Chapter 10	Dances, DJs and Dysentery	122
Chapter 11	Chas' Pirie Shows The Flag	131
Chapter 12	TOS Dhow to the Rescue	148
Chapter 13	The Empty Quarter	163
Chapter 14	Somebody had to Pay Them	173
Chapter 15	Wessex and Two Andovers	179
Chapter 16	The Joy of being a Trucial Oman Scout	192
Chapter 17	The View from the Air	199
Chapter 18	The TOS Boys School – My Story	207
Chapter 19	Reminiscences of a Radiographer	213
Chapter 20	Last Days	220
Chapter 21	The Last Hurrah	224

FOREWORD

Lt. General Sir John Macmillan KCB CBE

I was honoured when Terry invited me to write a Foreword to this wonderful collection of the memories of a very select band. Reading them through stirred my own recollection of a particularly happy time in my own military career. I missed out on the rugged life that the folk in the Squadrons enjoyed (or sometimes suffered?) Mirfa in mid-summer was OK for a night or two, but the air-conditioning in Sharjah had its attractions. Sadly my predecessor was in injury time, and I didn't have time for the Arabic course, so never got to know what the soldiers were saying except through my excellent orderly, Fred (Riza bin Ali) whose Arabic and English were both a bit suspect. At the time we lived for each day and enjoyed the freedom of being far from the MoD and even a good distance from our nearest masters in Bahrain.

I missed the most dramatic events: supporting SAF and the SAS in the Jebel Akhdar campaign, the transfer to pastures new of Sheikh Saqr of Sharjah, and Sheikh Shakhbut of Abu Dhabi, and the mutinies in Buraimi and in 'X' Squadron.

However much any of us thought about Lawrence of Arabia or Glubb Pasha in Jordan, we never imagined that we would be regarded, 40 years after the disbandment of the Scouts, as the founders of the great nation that the UAE has become. It was humbling to have this repeated many times over by our hosts when we were invited back to the Emirates in 2012. We had no idea that we were doing anything of more than local importance, stopping a scrap at the well at Ras al Khaimah or discouraging weapons smugglers helping the rebels in Oman. That the pupils in the Boys School would include future Generals never crossed our minds, but it was these young soldiers who became the leaders of their country. They and all the ex-Scouts who shared the early days with us showed their appreciation of our work so generously and so genuinely that our adventures in the sand all those years ago were given a whole new perspective.

Like so many of the contributors, I can only say, how lucky we were to be part of such a great story. .Congratulations to all who have helped us re-live those times, and especially to Terry and Hugh for bringing it all together.

John MacMillan

PREFACE

The Trucial Oman Scouts—a brief history

Allan Stanistreet RASC

The British have been in Treaty relations with the Rulers of the Gulf States since 1820. In exchange for their agreeing to refrain from piracy against British and East India Company ships, the British agreed to protect the tribes from any attacks by outsiders.

In May, 1853, all the Rulers signed a Perpetual Treaty of Peace, thus giving rise to a change of name from the Pirate Coast to the Trucial Coast. The Emirates concerned were, and still are, Abu Dhabi, Dubai, Sharjah, Ajman, Umm al Quwain, Ras al Khaimah and Fujeira.

During the 1930s, when air travel over long distances became possible for the more well-heeled living in the west, various staging posts were established on the air route to India, including one at Sharjah. This was run jointly by the Royal Air Force and Imperial Airways. A fort was built to accommodate travellers and this still exists, having been restored and converted into a fine museum.

Apart from the usual tribal differences of opinion, little of any note occurred until after World War Two, an event which barely touched the seven Sheikhdoms.

Between 1945 and 1950, exploratory drillings for oil took place. This involved the governments of Saudi Arabia, the Trucial States, Qatar and Oman, since the international borders were still ill-defined and everyone naturally had an interest in any oil revenues which might accrue. In 1949, matters came to a head and the British were obliged to intervene as a result of their treaty obligations to the Rulers of the Emirates. It was therefore necessary to form a paramilitary force, initially using recruits from the Jordanian Arab Legion. Preliminary discussions had taken place with a view to establishing this force between the Foreign Office and the Treasury and accordingly, in January, 1950, it was agreed to establish, 'a small armed force' in the Trucial States. Their duties were to protect the Political Officers in areas outside the Rulers' control; to assist the Rulers to maintain law and order and to attempt to suppress the slave trade[1] The name of the force was to be the Trucial Oman Levies (TOL) and, in number, was indeed modest, being commanded by a Major on contract from the Arab Legion (Major J.M. Hankin-Turvin) with thirty-five all ranks, detached from the Arab Legion, plus thirty men recruited locally. They were formally established by an Order in Council of 1950, but it was not until February 1951 that the main body arrived from Jordan. They were accommodated in part of the RAF camp at Sharjah. They brought with them from the Arab Legion that unit's distinctive red and white shemagh which was to distinguish the TOL and its successors until the end of their existence in 1976. The first local men were enlisted in February, 1951. As outlined above, the Levies were principally occupied in keeping the peace between the various tribes and patrolling vast areas of desert in an attempt to catch the slave traders. They had considerable success in both ventures and came to be highly regarded both by the Rulers and their subjects. Due to other Arab forces being unable to supply sufficient officers and trained soldiers, particularly in the technical arms, the force slowly built up its own cadre of British officers and soldiers over the years.

The uniform worn by the Levies consisted of a khaki drill (KD) shirt and trousers; red and white shemagh with black rope aqhul; brown leather sandals and 1938 pattern webbing. The cap badge was a single silver khanjar, or Arab dagger, worn in the aqhul. Commissioned officers and warrant officers wore a silver badge of crossed khanjas underneath which were two cannon and under those an inscription in Arabic: 'Force of the Coast of Oman'. Over time, further embellishments were added to the uniform, including a red lanyard and red stable belt. Officers and warrant officers also wore a small silver khanjar as collar dogs in their shirts.

In 1955, an incursion was made by the Saudis into disputed territory around Buraimi. Shots were exchanged and this developed into a full-blown operation, which was conducted in collaboration with the Sultan of Muscat's Armed Forces and the RAF. As a consequence of this operation, all ranks who participated were awarded the General Service Medal 1918-62 with clasp Arabian Peninsula, while an officer and two Arab NCOs were decorated for their gallantry in action: Captain Steggles was awarded the MC and Sergeant Mohammed Nakhaira bin Mahroum and Lance-Corporal Said Salim al Si'ar received the Military Medal. Also in 1956, Captain Sayid Mushon received a BEM and WO C Barnes a MBE. On 1 March, 1956 the name of the force was changed to Trucial Oman Scouts (TOS). Arms and equipment during this period and, indeed, for the entire existence of the force was more or less that for a British infantry battalion. Thus: .303 SMLE rifles, signal pistols, .38 Webley revolvers, .303 Bren light machine guns and two-inch mortars. The latter were soon discovered to provide inadequate firepower and they were replaced with three-inch mortars. Later on, .300 Browning medium machine guns were supplied. There were no heavy weapons.

An armoured car Squadron on detachment from the regiment in Aden was stationed in Sharjah. They were equipped with Ferret armoured cars and a Saladin, a much heavier, six-wheeled vehicle. This only left camp once. It immediately sank up to its belly in the soft sand, proving it was useless for operations. The British junior ranks messed with the armoured car Squadron. Scouts' vehicles consisted initially of Series I Land-Rovers, both short and long wheelbase, Morris one-ton trucks, mainly used as water bowsers and Bedford QL three-ton trucks. The latter were replaced by the Bedford RL in due course but a couple of the QLs lasted into the 1960s. In later days, some Dodge Power Wagons were introduced, which proved very popular and versatile.

When road vehicles were declared beyond economical repair by the REME workshops, they were sold off to the local civilians, who patched them up and used them for their own purposes, including as transport for passengers around the Emirates. Some of these vehicles had an incredibly long lifetime. To their great credit, the Army of the UAE has preserved some of these vehicles which are brought out on special occasions and demonstrated to visitors. They are preserved in their original liveries.

By the beginning of 1960, with Arab members outnumbering British volunteers by about ten to one, the strength of the TOS had reached 1153 all ranks, plus fifty boys, who were in training. Since the force was one of the very few places in the Emirates where children could learn to read and write, places in the Boys Squadron were popular and much sought after.
Many Arab generals started their careers in the TOS Boys School.

The Force Headquarters were at Sharjah. Eventually, the camp included a Medical Centre, Mechanical Transport Squadron, Signals Squadron and Quartermaster. All were mainly staffed by British officers and NCOs with Arab assistance. By now, Arab personnel had their own officers and NCOs, the majority of whom were proving to be very competent at their jobs. Also based in Sharjah was the dhobi and coffee shop, both owned and run by Esa bin Mousa al-Amri, an Iranian. He later sold the coffee shop to one of the Indian civilian staff, Mr G.B. Lulla. There was also a civilian camp shop owned by one Mr. Lalchand and managed by a Sikh: Hari Singh Bhatia. There were two clubs, one RAF and the other for TOS British personnel and the armoured car squadron. The Officers' Mess was in Sharjah, adjacent to the creek. The Sergeants' Mess was in the camp. In addition to the Training Squadron, which was based at Manama, there were five rifle Squadrons: A, 'B', 'C', 'D' and 'X,' the latter being composed entirely of Dhoffaris – superb soldiers. These rifle Squadrons rotated between the stations, which were variously Dhaid, Mirfa, Buraimi (Fort Jahili), Idhen and Sharjah.

In the early 1960's the Royal Army Pay Corps could not find sufficient volunteers among their regular soldiersto fill vacancies in the TOS. This resulted in five National Servicemen being asked if they would like to join us.

Discipline was never a problem because almost all British other ranks (BOR) were NCOs or warrant officers. A tough tour of duty lasted eighteen months, with six weeks inter-tour leave in a temperate climate. The main cause of early repatriation was usually ill health.

Sadly, a number of British personnel died while serving with the Scouts from one cause or another. Five were officers: Major H.O.D. Thwaites MC, 9th Lancers (killed in action 7 November 1953); Captain P. Chambers MC, Royal Hampshires (killed in action 28 March 1957); Lieutenant D. Rowarth RASC (killed in a traffic accident 1961); Lieutenant A. Aspinall RAMC (killed in a traffic accident 1961) and Major D.F.P. Tibbey MBE RAPC , 18 April 1968. The soldiers were: Signalman McNiff, April 1958; Corporal Adams REME, March 1964 and Corporal Day, Royal Corps of Signals, November 1964. Major Tibbey and Corporal Day are buried at the rear of the Christian church in Sharjah, where the small cemetery has recently been renovated by members of the Royal Navy.

At midnight on 22 December, 1971, the Trucial Oman Scouts passed into history, being replaced the following day by the Union Defence Force. It was still under the command of a British officer but Arab officers and soldiers were gradually taking over. The new organisation survived only a further five years before being completely reorganised in 1976 as the army of the United Arab Emirates as it is today. There are only a few recognisable locations now which are familiar to former British members of the Trucial Oman Scouts.

But that is not quite the end of the story. In 1989, a former soldier of the TOS, Terry Ward, decided to form an All Ranks Association. He contacted some of his former comrades and they held an informal get-together at a military club in London. There were seven members present: Terry Ward, Allan Stanistreet, John Hopkins, Dave Youell, Bruce Norman, Roger Davies and Bobby Cameron.

This organisation quickly grew and although time has inevitably taken its toll, the Association still holds regular reunions. In March 2012, in celebration of the sixtieth anniversary of the founding of the army of the UAE and the fortieth anniversary of the founding of the present state, sixty former members of the TOL, TOS and UDF were invited as guests of the Army of the UAE for a week in the Emirates, all expenses paid, to visit old haunts and meet old friends. It is, perhaps, an understatement to say that it was a most memorable trip. The hospitality was of the legendary Arab kind. Although there had been a few previous trips with smaller numbers, this was the icing on the cake.

From the time of our arrival, we were whirled round the Emirates, feasting as we went. Accommodation was five-star everywhere and nothing was too much trouble for our hosts. Almost everywhere we went, old soldiers turned out to greet us and it was really touching to see in how much respect and affection we British are held in this part of the world. Many of the party wore their shemaghs when out and about, resulting in requests for photographs from passers-by. On the last day, a Saturday, the morning was supposed to be a shopping day but the Ruler of Sharjah invited us to lunch. When the Ruler invites you to lunch – you go! This was the banquet to end all banquets in the most palatial surroundings imaginable with an immaculate table and excellent service from the staff. It was a memorable ending to a memorable trip. We shall go on with our meetings until we are no longer able to do so. Although we all represent different regiments and corps and for some this is the only military connection they maintain, we get on well together and now we are fortunate that some of our Arab friends are able to join us. As Terry Ward says, 'Anno domini will eventually take care of the Trucial Oman Scouts' Association!'

Bibliography

The Trucial Oman Scouts: The Story of a Bedouin Force by Michael Mann. Michael Russell (Publishing) Ltd, 1994.
Two Alpha Lima: The First Ten Years of the Trucial Oman Levies and Trucial Oman Scouts (1950 to 1960) by Peter Clayton. Janus, 1994.

Commanding Officers and Commanders of the Trucial Oman Levies, Trucial Oman Scouts and Union Defence Force
Maj J.M. Hankin-Turvin (Arab Legion contract officer) Jan 51 – Aug 53
Lt Col W.J. Martin OBE (Suffolk Regt) Aug 53 – Nov 54Lt
Col E.F. Johnston OBE MC (South Lancs Regt) Nov 54 – May 57
Col S.L.A. Carter OBE MC (Sherwood Foresters) May 57 – Mar 61
Col H.J. Bartholomew OBE (King's Own Border Regt) Mar 61 – Mar 64
Col F.M. de Butts CMG OBE (SCLI) Mar 64 – Feb 67
Colonel K.P.G. Ive OBE (17/21 Lancers) Feb 67 – May 70
Col H.R.C. Watson MBE (Queen's Regt) May 70 – Dec 71(Also commanded the UDF from Dec 71 – Mar 74)
Col K. Wilson MBE (Royal Scots) Mar 74 - Sep 74
Col R.H. Robinson OBE (R Anglian) Sep 74 - Dec 76

[1] Peter Clayton: Two Alpha Lima (Janus, 1994) preface

A newspaper headline in 1961

Exchange of gifts: Lt. Colonel Tim Courtenay, Lt. General Hamad Mohammed Thani al Ramethii (Chief of Defence Staff, UAE Armed Forces) and Lt. General Sir John Macmillan

Below: 60 British TOS Veterans return to Manama

MAPS OF THE REGION

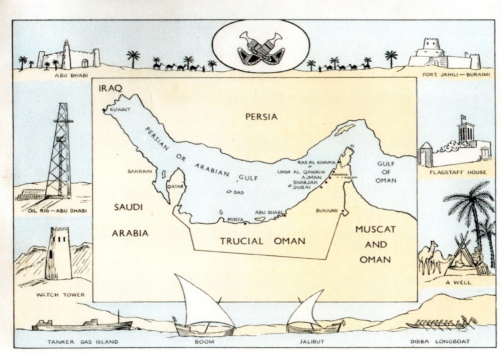

1

MUTINY AT BURAIMI OASIS

Bill Cruickshank REME

After surviving Korea, I was serving as a corporal in Egypt in 1953. One of our REME officers had his MG sports car shipped out from the UK. He asked me to work on it, more than once. I enjoyed this; it made a change from maintaining army trucks, etc. I would clean the body, the spark plugs, filters and the likes. One day he said to me.

'As a regular soldier, you probably know the old army saying never volunteer for anything.' From the way he spoke, I knew something was coming. He then went on to tell me about a new Foreign Office force that was being set up in the Trucial Oman. They were looking for volunteer REME officers and NCOs. Was I interested......? Once more unto the breach, dear friends.....this sounded rather different from normal soldiering, so I put my name down.

After some time had passed, I discovered that I had been accepted by the Trucial Oman Levies (TOL), and duly appeared before my CO. 'We are sorry to lose you' (they all say that). The RAF flew me to Hibbaniya, Iraq, where I met up with a REME Sergeant, Charlie Chinn, and Scouse Taylor, a REME lance corporal. Both had flown out from the UK and were going on the same assignment. We were told we were to fly to Bahrain, where we would be met by the British Political Advisor for the Persian Gulf. The 'bowler hat' told us a little about the new unit we were to join. It was called the Trucial Oman Levies at the time, but was shortly to be renamed, The Trucial Oman Scouts. It was an Arab force, trained and led by a handful of British officers and NCOS and based at a place called Sharjah in the Trucial States. We hadn't a clue where that was. Its mission, apparently, was, amongst other things, to protect the seven Sheikhdoms who were friendly to the UK, from intruders and border incursions.

We set out on another 'plane journey. This time in an RAF Anson, a canvas covered, twin-engine aircraft; arriving in Sharjah on the 28th April 1953.

The camp was adjacent to a twentieth century building with a fort-like edifice, owned and run by Cable and Wireless. We were to live in billets that had been used by the RAF during the Second World War. A small detachment of RAF personnel were still stationed there to service the Anson. The airfield, primitive though it was, could handle larger planes, and very occasionally a Dakota would stop off on its way from India to Saudi Arabia.

Our commanding officer was Lieutenant Colonel Martin of the Suffolk Regiment. British army captains acted as company commanders. We three REME types were responsible to an admin officer who, by and large, left us to get on with it. The only available vehicles were a few old Land Rovers and a three ton Bedford truck. It was up to us to keep them running. This wasn't easy, because spare parts were non-existent. We had to use items retrieved from wherever we could get them; often resorting to cannibalising 'dead' vehicles. We were eventually provided with a few more Land Rovers and Morris one-tonners. In typical army fashion, they arrived, painted green and fitted with snow and mud tyres!

It was months before suitable sand tyres arrived. Until then, whenever we drove into the desert and came to soft sand, we were obliged to deflate the tyres. We had a rather neat device for re-inflating them. This consisted of a modified spark plug with an air hose attached to it. One of the vehicle's spark plugs was removed and the air valve plug was screwed into the engine. Start it up and the cylinder compression inflated the tyre...easy.

I soon fell in love with the desert, enjoying the challenge of driving on tracks that were frequently obscured by the shifting sand. There were no tarmac' roads in Trucial Oman. One of the manned outposts was at a distant oasis called Buraimi. Equipped with whatever spares we could lay our hands on and carrying plenty of water, Charlie Chinn and I would make the difficult journey there in Morris one-tonners, in order to service the vehicles at the fort. We would hang goatskin water bags on the outside of our trucks; evaporation through the skin keeping the barely drinkable liquid cool. We carried lemonade powder (army issue) as a mixer to improve its taste. Leaving Sharjah in the afternoon, we would head out across the desert. The going was firm as we left the coast, crossing a stony, shrub covered landscape.

TOL on parade at Sharjah camp

We would plan to get to the dune country by the late afternoon then wait for the cool of the evening when the surface of the sand became a little damp, and consequently, slightly firmer. With no roads or tracks, the fun would start as we negotiated this natural barrier that always seemed to do its best to prevent us from reaching our destination. We carried sand channels, approx. eight feet long and four wide. These were metal sheets with holes cut in them in a regular pattern. Essential pieces of equipment for this type of terrain, they had been around ever since man first ventured into the desert using an internal combustion engine. If, or rather when you get bogged down, the sheets are placed in front of the stuck wheels. Then, after digging them out as best you can, you slide the sheets under the wheels, then drive forward as fast as possible. Once the truck is clear, you retrieve the sheets and carry on until you, inevitably, need them again. It is exhausting work, and one of the reasons why you never went into the blue (the desert) on your own.

The fort at Buraimi Oasis

Once over the barrier, we would bed down until first light. Sometimes we had very little sleep. On one occasion, both trucks became so bogged down in dune country, even the metal sheets were of no use to us.

When daylight came and that killer of a sun began to climb, we took shelter beneath a truck. We had water and were fairly confident that we would be all right because an RAF Anson flew the route every day, looking for intruders. It was bound to spot us. And it did. Not wishing to suffer the ignominy of being rescued, we picked ourselves up and struggled manfully to free our vehicles until, at last, we succeeded.

By the time we got to Buraimi, the troops were getting ready to come to our assistance. We had spent only one day 'out there', but our lips were raw and our eyes sore from the wind blown sand. Nevertheless, Beau Geste William, loved every minute he spent in the desert. In those days it took about twenty four hours to travel from Sharjah to Buraimi. Today, one can cover the distance in a couple of hours on a super-highway.

Morris one-tonners. In typical army fashion they arrived, painted green and fitted with snow and mud tyres!

As time went by, we received even more new Land Rovers and Bedford 4x4s. We also had an Austin recovery truck. Its winch came in very handy, especially in the rainy season when large areas of the desert would flood; lakes of water appearing within a matter of hours. Our Arab drivers had little experience of driving on dry sand, let alone wet. They, of course, were more used to travelling on foot, or on donkeys or camels. Many would keep their foot on the accelerator until the vehicle they were driving was up to its axles in sand. It took us two whole days to get one of them out of soft sand. At certain times of the year, we were given sacks of poisoned bran to use for locust control. I believe this came from the UN Locust Commission. A swarm of locusts is a fantastic sight. Another one is a fast moving sandstorm. The fiercest of them could easily strip the paint off a truck.

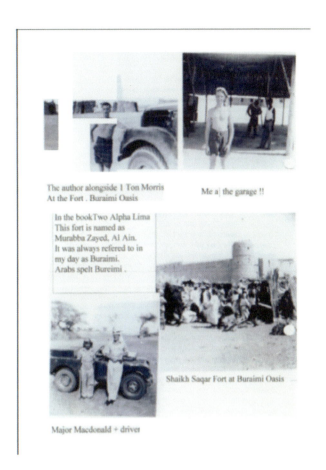

The author alongside 1 Ton Morris At the Fort. Buraimi Oasis

Me at the garage !!

In the book Two Alpha Lima This fort is named as Murabba Zayed, Al Ain. It was always refered to in my day as Buraimi. Arabs spelt Bureimi.

Shaikh Saqar Fort at Buraimi Oasis

Major Macdonald + driver

The Buraimi Incident

On the 5th of November 1953, Charlie and I had gone, as usual, to do the regular truck inspections and maintenance at Buraimi. The day after we arrived, we heard a lot of shouting and saw rifles being waved about by the Levies, who were mostly recruits from Aden. Someone told us they were on the point of mutiny. With no idea of what was really going on, we carried on working; no one had told us to do otherwise.

That night, Major Thwaites told us that his Squadron was being recalled to Sharjah. He said that many of the Adeni Levies had been selling rifle bullets to the local Arabs.

The next morning, when we got up for breakfast, Major Thwaites ordered Charlie and me to prepare for trouble. I looked at Charlie and he looked at me. TROUBLE, EH!!

The major returned later on and ordered us to go with him, along with Doctor Duncan of the RAF, and Sergeant Major Daoud. We were to apprehend three Adeni Levies who had refused orders from their officer to return to base.

We were to go unarmed in order to show them that our intentions were peaceful. After all, there were five of us and only three of them.

Sketch map showing the position of the Fort and Post 5

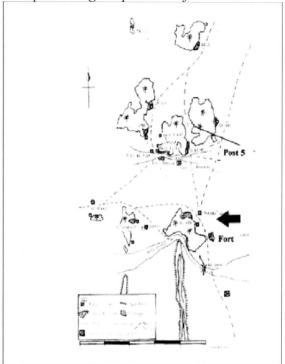

As we drove to Post 5, which was some way out, we saw the Levies in question walking along the track, away from their ordered position. Major Thwaites stopped his vehicle and walked up to them, accompanied by the doctor and Daoud. He signed for us to join them. I heard Dauod shout at the three Levies. They stopped walking as we approached them, then suddenly and without warning, opened up on us with their rifles. I saw the major and Duncan fall to the ground. Daoud turned to run towards us but was also hit. Unarmed, Charlie and I began running towards our Morris. Charlie fell to the ground as bullets struck him. I carried on towards the truck. I'd never run so fast in all my life. I jumped into the back of the Morris. We always carried spare petrol in a fifty or sixty gallon drum. I lay there beside one of them, thinking, it's only a matter of time now. I've had it. Bullets were ripping through the truck's canvas top and straight into the drum of petrol. I was getting covered in the stuff. Any minute now! As I passed out from the effect of the fumes, I remember saying to myself, 'When my mum's told I've been killed, she'll say, 'He died on his father's birthday.' It was, too. He had been born on 7th November 1907.

I returned to consciousness and became aware that the truck was moving at high speed. I had no idea who was at the wheel. When it stopped at the fort, I jumped out and saw that the driver was Charlie! How he'd managed to do it, severely wounded as he was, was quite astonishing to me. I remember shouting,

'Stand to the legion!' What a damn fool thing to say.

A Trucial Oman Levies officer came over to me. My head was bleeding as a result of being struck by fragments of the petrol drum. I was also soaked in the stuff. I told him what had happened and asked him to go and recover the bodies.

Upon entering the fort, I discovered that Charlie had already contacted Sharjah by radio. He had been told to await further orders. It was a Saturday. Charlie's arm was in a serious condition; several bones were shattered.

We went to the room at the top of the fort, where I applied a rough tourniquet. Charlie lay down after I'd bandaged his shattered arm. I noticed then that his shirt was becoming soaked in blood. Turning him over, I saw that part of his side was split wide open. I applied pressure to the wound until the bleeding stopped. What a bloody mess we were in!

When the Arab officer returned, I told him in no uncertain terms that no one was to enter the fort and climb the stairs to our room. If they did, I would shoot them. I tied two magazines together, then loaded a gun. I felt unable to trust any of the Arab Levies at the time, including this officer.

A very long night began. Charlie was great; he never moaned at all. In fact, he said how lucky we'd been to get away. I sat there thinking, 'We're not in the clear yet, Charlie.'

Back at base, they had only a vague idea about our true situation. They knew about the previous day's unrest among the Levies, now they'd received a message telling them that the British officers were dead and some NCOs were severely wounded.

The commander decided to drive overnight to Buraimi with a trustworthy company of Levies, await first light, then advance and disarm those at the fort.

Charlie and I knew nothing of this, we just waited – and waited. At first light, I heard the Anson circling overhead, so I went to the roof of the fort and waved like hell.

Soon after that, I saw the Land Rovers approaching, with Major Macdonald in the leading one. The dead were loaded onto the Anson, along with Charlie. I was obliged to wait until I had reported to the Colonel. His first words to me were,

'Cruickshank, where's your beret!?' (British NCOs had not been issued with shemaghs at the time.)

After reporting the events, I am not at all sure how I got back to base. It was probably by Anson. I do remember climbing into my bed, falling asleep, then being awakened by someone who wanted to hear the story. I told him to go and jump in the lake….if he could find it!

Within days of the shooting, the three mutineers were handed over by a local sheikh. They had asked for his protection but he'd refused to give it. The majority of the remaining Adenis were discharged and flown back to Aden.

I had to wait several months for the trial of the three mutineers to take place. This was due to the fact that the mutiny had occurred in a disputed border area. Eventually, the Sultan of Muscat won the right to hold the trial. It was about this time that my promotion to sergeant came through.

For no good reason, I was flown to Bahrain and checked over at the hospital there. The Matron came from Aberdeen. She said I could stay in her apartment rather than the RAF camp. I had four or five super days or rather nights; they seemed to party every time the sun went down; although, by law, Bahrain was a very dry state indeed! We often went to Awali, the oil company town on the island. Soon after I arrived in Bahrain, I had met the chief of police of the island. He asked me what I was doing for transport. I hadn't given it a thought.

'Come to the police station for your driving test,' he suggested.

On Parade at Fort Jahili

I was provided with a Land Rover and told to drive round the block. After doing so, he handed me a driving licence and told me to look after the vehicle.

'Bring it back to me before you leave for Sharjah.'

The matron gave me a pile of Neville Shute's books to take back to Sharjah. Everyone was so kind to me.

It was May or June 1954 before the trial of the mutineers took place. It was to be held in Muscat. I wanted to get the whole thing over and done with, but until then, I carried on with my work, much as before.

Charlie's mother lived in Camborne, Cornwall. I wrote to her and received a nice letter in return. She wrote that Charlie had been flown to England. His arm was now encased in a leather bandage. It was remiss of me, but I never did keep in touch with him. If he had not driven that truck, wounded as he was, I could well have died. What a heel I was!

Things started to change. Many more local Arabs were recruited and the rest of the Adenis were returned to Aden. A new man was put in charge of our REME unit. I think his name was Dodds; we certainly called him DoDo.

At last the trial got underway. The journey to Muscat was made overnight. We stopped at the Sultan's army camp, had a meal then drove on to Muscat. I was to stay with a member of the British Embassy staff. His wife very kindly did my washing and cooking. I spent a great deal of time walking around the city. It was very old and customs had not changed there for centuries. For example, if you went out at night, you had, by law, to carry a lamp or some other form of light. You were liable to be arrested if you were found without one. It was explained to me that if you had no light, you were up to no good! I did enjoy walking through the small alleyways.

Muscat has mountains quite close to the rear of the town. The sun's heat is somehow held by them and reflected back into the town at night. The prison stood on a cliff overlooking the harbour. It must have been some sort of hell in there.

The trial was all a bit of a mystery to me because it was conducted in Arabic. When I was questioned, my answers were translated back and forth. The three mutineers were found guilty and sent to the prison. They could not be executed for murder, because the only witness available was a Christian...me!

Not long after the trial, I started my journey back to the UK. The first leg was by 'plane to the Canal Zone in Egypt. Once I got there, I was to wait in the tented, transit camp. How long I waited I cannot remember. More than once, I was driven to the airport, only to be told, 'Sorry, flight full.' I did eventually get on a York aircraft of RAF Transport Command. We landed at Cyprus for refuelling, then went on to Stanstead, in Essex. I remember flying over the green fields of England and thinking how I had forgotten how lovely grass was.

E

Engine change Morris one-tonner

Cpl Stan Guscin REME-in the early days, before a TOS uniform was established

I travelled to the REME HQ at Arborfield, where I was issued with new kit and a travel warrant to get me home. I went to my Auntie Beanie, who lived in Caversham Road, Kentish Town, in London. She didn't recognise me at first, then told me that I'd better send my mum a telegram letting her know that I was home. I didn't do that – I wanted to surprise her.

My Auntie Ethel lived next door to mother. I went to her place first, so that she could break the news of my homecoming to her. Ethel shouted out of the window to get mother's attention. She was in the wash house at the time. 'Your loon's hame!'

They all started crying...yes, I was home. I had about sixty days leave and no idea what it had in store for me, nor for a wee girl called Margaret Beattie Wilson.

The view from the fort to Jebel Hafit

TOS Signals' Centre. No. 19 Wireless set.
All communications were made by Morse Code

2

CODES, ROADS AND REBELS

Trevor Harding Royal Signals

   I was on my way back to Saighton Camp in Cheshire, when a figure coming towards me revealed himself to be Corporal Ed Newberry, who, six months earlier, had beaten me to a posting to Nigeria because he had a valid passport.
  'Hi, Ed. I didn't expect to see you! What are you doing back here?'
  'I'm working behind the bar in the Officers' Mess, waiting for a posting. The OC was talking to me a few days ago; he's going to replace a guy selected for the TOS, with me.'
  'Like hell he is. I'm the guy you're talking about!'
  'Sorry, Trev. The wheels are already in motion.'

The following day, the RSM sent for me.

'Corporal Harding, the OC would like to speak with you.'

Minutes later, that very man started to build a case to justify his giving the posting to Ed rather than me. I interrupted him, insisting I was going to be the chosen one.

''Ere,' said the RSM. 'You can't speak to your commanding officer like that.'

'It's quite all right, sergeant major', the OC said, 'let him have his say.'

The outcome was - Ed stayed behind the bar for a little longer. Such are the vagaries of life.

TOS Headquarters

As soon as the pilot slid the door open a blast of hot air hit me. A Land Rover pulled up. Its driver was wearing a smart uniform - and a turban. I grabbed my gear and went down the aircraft steps. After introductions, the driver advised me that he was already a few weeks overdue for demob and that I was his replacement. He went on to inform me that there was a joint RAF/TOS cypher room within the control tower building. It was manned on a twenty four hours on, twenty four hours off, basis. There was also a cypher room next to the TOS Signals' Centre. My, soon to depart, colleague was a great guy and we got on well together.

After completing the 'rounds', collecting uniforms, etc, I went to meet the TOS commander, Colonel Carter. Formidable! We returned to the billet to meet the lads. They were a great crew, including one nicknamed, 'Ying Tong'; he was quite a character among characters.

With some trepidation, I agreed to take over in the cypher room.

I 'won my spurs' at breakfast the next day. After eating a couple of spoonfuls of cereal, one of the lads casually asked me,

'What's that floating on top of the milk?' I looked down at the bits floating about in the reconstituted liquid.

'Just bits,' I replied.

'[No, they're not just bits, mate. They look like they're swimming.' I looked a little closer. Yes, the bits were swimming, all right. But I continued eating.

'You'll do us', the lads said. And I already felt part of the outfit.

I was on duty when the chap I had replaced departed, but I went and saw him off. Eight or ten officers, including Colonel Carter, formed a gangway to the aircraft to bid him farewell. I was deeply impressed by that. I simply couldn't imagine that happening elsewhere in the British army.

By the time about eight weeks had passed, my RAF colleague and I were coping well, then, suddenly, having virtually lost his sight, he was casevaced to a military hospital in Aden. Our RAF Medical Officer suspected the man had a brain tumour.

Now working night and day, in our fully operational cypher office, I resorted to trying to get some sleep on a mattress that I placed on the communications room floor. A few days later I had a throat problem and made a quick visit to the MO, whose office was not far away from where I worked.

'You've got laryngitis.'
He gave me some very large sweets to suck and told me to take three days off duty.
'Can't do it,' I said. 'You've just casevaced my RAF colleague to Aden. I'm on my own.'
He increased my bag of sweets from small to very large, and told me to keep sucking away.

The Cable and Wireless Building

I had been working non-stop for a number of days and, on this particular day, had missed lunch and tea, so I used the TOS duty vehicle to go and get some food that I could eat while working. The following day, I managed to get back to my billet for a shower and change of clothes. The lads asked where the hell I'd been, joking that they were going to report me AWOL. Did I know that I'd been put on a charge? I explained about the current lack of manpower in the cypher room then made my way to Warrant Officer Tyler's office to try and get the charge dropped. I asked him who had charged me with mis-use of a vehicle, i.e., the Land Rover I'd used to go and buy some food in a hurry. Tyler said he couldn't tell me, and I would have to attend CO's orders the following morning. The next day, I left the cypher room unattended again and made my way to the admin block. After I'd explained the situation to the RSM, he came with me to see the duty officer. Once in front of him, I let fly with both barrels about the sheer stupidity of it all. He got the message and ordered the RSM to delete the charge from all records. I dashed back to the cypher room.

I continued working alone for many days until an RAF replacement arrived from Bahrain. As soon as he turned up, I asked him to dump his kit and take over; I needed to get some sleep! Later on, I analysed the amount of traffic I had handled during this period. In one twenty four hour shift, it was in excess of forty thousand words. The next busiest amounted to thirty six thousand; the average being over twenty four thousand words per shift.

My new RAF colleague had been in Bahrain for a number of years but still found the Sharjah heat difficult to cope with. Used to having colleagues working alongside him, he kept sending a runner for me at various times of the day and night. The lads repeatedly told me to, 'Let him sort it out himself.'

Colonel Stuart Carter. Formidable!
Commander of the TOS

About eight of us arrived at the open air cinema one evening and started to file into one of the rows. I said that I needed to be on the outside, in case I was called upon.

My friends insisted that I took an inside seat. Halfway through the film, a runner arrived and shouted out,

'Corporal Harding, please report to the RAF Communication Centre!'

I tried to get up, but two pairs of hands held me to my seat and two voices whispered,

'Let the bugger sort it out himself.'

I relaxed. What else could I do?

A quarter of an hour later, and the runner came back with the same call. The same process was repeated. A shorter period of time elapsed, then, there he was again, with the same request. This time his voice was an octave higher. He had obviously been threatened with dire consequences if he didn't come back with me. As I told the lads that I would have to go, one of the RAF officers at the back, got to his feet and shouted,

'For God's sake!' I heard a voice, which I think belonged to Wing Commander Gillies, telling him to sit down.

When I arrived at the cypher room, my RAF colleague advised me that I was in trouble, 'Big trouble'

'How come?' I asked.

It transpired that we had received a flash message that was 'mine', and it should have been decoded and acted upon an hour earlier– that's why I was in, 'Big, big trouble'. I pointed out that he was the duty cryptographer, not me. I cut short the argument about the pros and cons of the situation and asked him for the message. When I looked at it, I saw what the problem was. Neither he, nor I, had worked on that particular code before. I was quite certain, though, that it was not, after all, 'one of mine'. My RAF colleague said that we should contact the wing commander immediately. To which I retorted,

'With all due respect, what the hell can he do?'

We opened the safe and got out every code book we had. As I went through them, I discarded the obvious, leaving a small pile which I split between the two of us. We finished examining them without result and swapped piles to check that neither of us had missed what we were looking for. I got through the first few books - then 'eureka', I'd got it! My colleague came over, looked down and said,

'That doesn't mean anything to me.'

I told him that I'd cracked it, but for one horrible moment I 'lost it' again. I thought hard, recalled what it was, and continued until the decoding was complete. We were able to laugh when we discovered that no-one was waiting for the message, after all. It was for 'our eyes only'. Escaped again!!

The RAF cypher clerk was eventually replaced by three RAF cryptographers, all sergeants, enabling us to go on to a three shift system.

Everything was going well, except I that I couldn't get to sleep properly. My brain refused to switch off. I went to see our great Scottish Medical Officer and explained what was happening. He gave me a little pill, changed his mind and gave me two.

'Take those and you will sleep like a baby.'

I returned to the billet, took the pills and sat on my bed, talking to 'Benny' Goodman and Mike Fields, feeling drowsy,

'Sorry guys. I've got to lie down.'

I woke up the next morning in time for my shift, with my head in a sort of cloud, a condition which stayed with me for a couple of days.

I went on my first trip up country, to Manama. There were just two vehicles. The lead Land Rover contained Captain Fisher, plus others. My friend 'Taffy' drove the other one, with me and two other junior NCOs as passengers. We came to some shifting sand hills. The lead vehicle got over them without any difficulty. As we approached them, I advised Taffy to put his foot down. He didn't, and we bogged down half way up a dune. We dug ourselves out, reversed down, and tried again. Taffy put his foot down this time, and up we went until we almost reached the summit. For some reason best known to Taffy, he took his foot off the accelerator- and we bogged down again. So- we dug ourselves out, reversed down, even further than the last time- and tried
again.

Once an impregnible fortress

Taffy was doing well! We raced up the dune, reached the summit - then we were airborne! Taffy didn't take his foot off the gas at all this time! We crash landed on the other side of the dune; the doors flew open, jerry cans of water and petrol whizzed through the air; likewise those NCOs sitting in the back. I was, for a moment, very disorientated, then realised that I was almost upside down with my legs draped over the dashboard and on to the Land Rover's bonnet. We regrouped. Taffy was OK. The other two guys were OK-ish. After saying a prayer of thanks, we put everything back in order. Taffy and I, having glanced towards the other Land Rover, which was some way off, saw that its occupants were highly amused. When we caught up with them they said it had all looked rather spectacular.

The RAF organised excursions to the beach from time to time. Unfortunately, one such trip ended tragically. A number of lives were lost when a freak wave engulfed the party of swimmers and sunbathers. One of my wireless operator friends was with them. Although he was a very good swimmer himself, he told me that he had only just survived the wave and could do nothing to save any of the others.

DH Venom fighter   *AVRO Shackleton bomber*

I was persuaded to go on one of the monthly payroll runs with Corporal Alan Whittaker and the paymaster. Just prior to setting out, I visited the TOS Signals Centre and happened to glance at a message a wireless operator was receiving. It was headed 'secret'. I made a mental note to have a quiet word with the outstation officer concerned

Upon our arrival at the camp in question, we sat down to our evening meal, which, almost inevitably, was a heaped plate of curry. I noticed that the food on the plate of the officer on my right seemed to be moving. Everyone else, including the officer himself, could hardly avoid noticing this strange phenomenon. Very slowly, a large dung beetle emerged from the depths of his curry. The officer casually flicked the thing on to the floor and revealed to us that he'd had an argument with the cook that day. When the orderly came to collect the plates, he told him to inform the cook that the meal had been very nice. Well done that man!
We then got in to a general discussion, during which I brought up the question of the 'secret', un-coded, message I had seen.
'It was sent in code - Morse code,' someone said.
What could I say to that, other than the obvious; Morse code was an international means of efficient communication, but Morse networks were easily capable of being monitored by others. We spoke about the problem the TOS were having in communicating classified information quickly. The only means of transferring classified or secret messages at that time was via a Land Rover, or other vehicle.

The RAF had eight Venom fighters and four Shackleton bombers stationed at Sharjah. Early one evening, having just been to the control tower ablutions, I noticed that the paraffin lamps on the runway had been lit, so I wandered over to see what was happening. I leant on one of the oil drums which surrounded the perimeter of the runway, and was joined by the fire chief. When I asked him why the flares were lit, he told me that a Shackleton was coming in late. After a time, we saw aircraft lights in the distance, then the landing lights, when they were switched on.
There was a rush of blood to my head when I saw what was happening to the approaching 'plane.
'He's coming in too low and too fast!'
'He'll be alright,' the chief reassured me.

Seconds passed, then we both became frozen to the spot as the Shackleton slammed onto the runway of packed sand, then sprang about thirty feet back into the air. The pilot reacted very quickly. With all four engines on full throttle the 'plane clawed its way back into the sky. After gaining height, the pilot completed a circuit of the airfield and came in for a perfect landing.
 Others were not so lucky. One of the Venom fighter pilots, shortly after taking off on a sortie, reported to the control tower that he had a problem. He jettisoned his fuel and came in to land, but crashed at the end of the runway. This incident was followed by another crash a few days later. A third one happened within a few days of that. This time, the pilot was said to have contacted the control tower and stated that something was flapping about on the 'plane. He had thought it might have been the hatch cover to his ammunition loading point. Although he'd said that he intended to jettison fuel, he failed to do so. No more was heard from him.

Cpl Trevor Harding; escort for Paymaster

When a search and recovery party went out, they found the piece of the aircraft that contained the hatch cover. It was closed and intact. One of the off-duty wireless operators was a member of the search party. He told me how he had come across part of a human arm sticking out of a sand dune. The person in charge of the search came over, examined the find, and suggested they pull the body out. My RAF colleague had taken hold of the arm, but there had been no body attached to it beneath the sand. He became very subdued after that experience.
  The squadron leader, suspecting that the crashes had been caused by sabotage, suspended flying operations and gave me a message for encoding before sending it to the War Office, informing them of his decision.
  A few hours later, I received a return message. The War Office had not been at all happy about his decision, or the fact that he had not sought their permission before making it.

I was rather shocked by the harsh tone of the message, because, to my mind, the squadron leader had made the only decision possible. Aware that he was in the briefing room, outlining some plan of action to his senior NCOs, I decided that I ought to try and get him out of there, so that I could show him the message in private.

There was no-one on duty outside the door. When I turned its handle and gave it a push, it didn't move; so I put my shoulder against it and felt resistance from the other side. Someone was leaning on it to prevent anyone gaining access. When I pushed harder, a sergeant popped his head round the door; I didn't know him, or he me. He saw my TOS uniform, and whispered,
'You're not allowed in here. Go away.'
I whispered back, 'Yes, I am.'
'No, you're not,' he said, and tried to shut the door on me. Feeling that I had no other option, I shoulder charged the door. The sergeant staggered back, allowing me to enter the room. The squadron leader looked towards the disturbance and asked if I wanted to see him. Moving to the front of the briefing room, I gave him the message. He read it and stood in silence for a moment. Then I whispered, 'Sorry about this, sir.' After a pause, he whispered back,
'It's okay, corporal.' Then he signed for the message - and everything was back to normal.

RAF Venom on a low-level strafing run

Shortly after that happened, we had a visitor from the War Office; no less a personage than an air vice marshal; he was either fact finding, pouring oil on troubled waters, or both. The cypher room bell rang and I opened the hatch. It was the man himself.
'Corporal, would you see that this message goes to the War Office?' I took it from him. It was a 'situation report'
'Certainly, sir.' I was about to close the hatch, but he seemed to be hovering, so I asked, 'Is there something else, sir?'
'Yes, I'd like to come in and watch you work.'
'Sorry, sir, you're not allowed in here.'
'But I have clearance up to and including cabinet office level.'
'That may be, sir, but you haven't got clearance for this office.'
He didn't know whether to laugh or cry, so settled for a gracious smile.
'I can request clearance for you, if you wish, sir.'
'No, it's all right, corporal. I won't be here that long.'

'One back for the squadron leader,' I thought.

Early one morning, around 0100 hours, I was called from the cypher room to the communication room. One of the wireless operators had been scanning radio frequencies and had picked up a 'Mayday' call, together with a request for the British Legation in Dubai. The operator had been trying to get positive identification on what or who was sending out the distress signal, but without success. Our link with the legation was closed for the night. I could clearly hear the 'Mayday' call myself, but we received no response to our identification requests. I made the decision to go to the legation, taking the wireless operator who had the frequency and other details, with me. The TOS duty driver stopped at the guardhouse and went inside to report where he was taking us. The orderly sergeant didn't believe a word of it and came out to check for himself. A quick explanation from me and off we went.

It was a black night, so I could only hope the driver knew the way and we didn't get bogged down; he did, and we didn't.

When we arrived at the legation, I knocked loudly on the door. There was no response, so I knocked again. When that didn't work, I resorted to chucking gravel at one of the top windows, hoping it didn't break the glass. A head emerged.

'What do you want?'

I told the head about the 'Mayday' call, gave it other details and suggested that it made contact with whoever was in distress.

'Right-oh,' the head replied, and disappeared from view without even a thank you.

TOS Squadron leaving Sharjah for the Jebel Akhdar

I was just coming off an RSM Parade briefing about an exercise we were going on when one of my signals colleagues came running up to me.

'Trev, we've been put on a charge!'

'Who's we?' I asked.
'Me, you and Ginger. Somebody's reported us for being late on parade.'
'I can't believe it. Who said so?'
'The staff sergeant……'
We hadn't been late on parade, so I spoke to the RSM.
'Excuse me, sir, have you put us on a charge?'
'No. What would I do that for?'
'For being late on parade, sir.'
'But I saw you were there on time. Who's made the charge?'
'Staff Sergeant………..'
'Forget it, corporal. Leave it with me.'

Views of old Dubai

Before coming off duty the following day, Ginger, who was in the TOS Signals Centre, told me what he'd witnessed. The RSM had turned up at the Signals Centre.
'Staff Sergeant; why have you put three signals corporals on a charge?'
'Because they were late on parade, sir.'
'No they weren't, staff.' 'Yes, they were, sir.'
'Are you calling me a liar, staff sergeant?' And so on.
It eventually emerged that the signals officer, had, for some mysterious reason, called the staff sergeant into his office and ordered him to put us on a charge. What can one say!?

When time permitted, I participated in football matches against Sharjah. The games were always competitive and usually ended with a close result. Thinking it would be an easy game to play, I also tried my hand at hockey; playing against 'C' Company, the Cameronians. How wrong can you be! I came off the pitch utterly exhausted.

Jebel Akhdar a 10,000 ft high rebel stronghold

Just in passing, when I first arrived in Sharjah, the bread was rank, due to weevil infestation. It was completely inedible on its own, so we used to spread thick layers of margarine and jam on it, take a deep breath, then bite and swallow.

There was a problem further up the gulf. I decoded a flash message for the OC of our support company, the Kings. They had been put on a one hour standby and had a frigate standing off Dubai to uplift them, if required. It was 0300 hours.

I jumped into the duty Land Rover and directed the driver to the guardhouse. Once there, I asked the guard commander for the location of the OC's accommodation.
'I don't have a clue where he's billeted,' he replied.
'Well, who does know?' I asked.

'I don't know! Won't your orderly room sergeant know?'
'He could do! Can you get him on the 'phone and ask him to get here as quick as he can?'
When the orderly sergeant appeared, I asked him where his OC's billet was.
'Sorry, I don't know, but I'll take the message, corporal.'
'No, you won't. Does your RSM know his location?'
'There's a good chance he does.'
'Okay, sarge, jump in the Land Rover and take me to him, the clock is ticking.'

We woke the RSM up.
'Could you tell me the location of your OC, sir?'
'Not exactly; but I do know which block he's in, and roughly which billet he uses. Leave it to me. I'll take the message for you, corporal.'
'Sorry, sir. I need your OC.'
'Oh! It's like that is it?'
'Yes, sir.'
I knocked on the door behind which the RSM had suggested I would find the OC, and hoped it was the right one.

It was, and the major was seriously out of sorts at being woken up in the early hours of the morning; even more so when he saw me standing in front of him in my TOS uniform. 'I have an urgent message for you, sir.'
He took it from me, read its contents, looked at the date and time of the message, then at his watch, and puffed himself up into a rage.
'Where the hell have you been, corporal!?'
I told him politely that I had decoded the message and knew its contents. I also pointed out that I had seen his guard commander, orderly sergeant and RSM before finding someone who knew his location. He deflated. 'Thank you, corporal.'
I returned to the communications room.

This is not the book in which to write about the complexities of the Jebel Akhdar campaigns. Suffice to say that the area was a rebel stronghold and due to the combination of their tenacity and the impossible terrain, it was proving difficult to dislodge them. At an RSM briefing we were told to kit up for an operation lasting three to four weeks.
We set off a few days later. I had been informed by a colleague that our column numbered around forty vehicles of various types. Our objective was a location close to Jebel Akhdar. This, the grapevine had said, would be reached by a feint that would take our column a number of miles past the area before doubling back to it.

We continued on until evening, then stopped to have a break and refuel, etc. Retracing our tracks at a fast rate of knots, we turned in the direction of the jebel (mountains). It was essential we reached it by 0400 hours.
All went well until the early hours of the morning. My vehicle was approximately mid-way in the column.

As my driver, Mohammed, negotiated a sharp, double bend, sloping steeply downwards, our rear wheels slewed alarmingly enough to make me lean forward so that I could use our wing mirror to check on the vehicle behind us. When I did, I was just in time to see it slide off the dune and disappear from sight. Mohammed also saw it. He looked across at me and I signalled him to stop. I'm thinking that we might be able to help drag the Bedford out from wherever it had ended up. These hopes were dashed when one of the officers in the convoy turned up to tell me that it was an ammunition truck that had gone off the track. A vehicle fitted with a winch arrived and attempted to drag the lorry back onto firmer ground, such as it was. Unfortunately, when the winching started, it was the winch vehicle that was dragged towards the ammunition truck. There was nothing for it but to lighten the lorry by unloading the ammunition. After it had finally been winched out, the lorry had to be reloaded again, all in complete darkness. We had lost a lot of time. Prior to starting off again, one of the officers had asked me if I knew where we were heading.

'No, sir, I don't.'

'That's okay,' he said, 'just stay on this track until you reach a junction. Turn left when you get there, and keep on going.'

We arrived at the junction and took the left fork. Great! It was now an easy run. Straight on, then another junction appeared. Mohammed stopped the vehicle. I jumped down to examine the track under the light of a match. Mohammed joined me and we quickly decided which track to follow. Our decision was confirmed as being the right one, by the same officer as before. We continued on to our objective as fast as we could.

False dawn was upon us as we turned a corner between sand dunes. The back of another Bedford three tonner was suddenly there. We come to a grinding halt just behind it. As soon as I jumped from the cab I was confronted by one of the occupants who appeared to be beside himself with anger.

'Where the hell have you been? Don't you know we have to be in position by 0400 hours!?' I'm tired and can't be bothered to reply. I simply looked at him. My officer friend tells him that it's not my fault. I had stopped to assist a vehicle in trouble.

We finally arrived at our destination and got settled in.

Sometime during the course of the operation, my colleague and I were at a falaj tank, having a wash and shave. We all used Silvikrin shampoo to wash with. It was the only form of soap that would lather when we were obliged to use salt water. Two Arab women were nearby, washing some clothes. Suddenly, one of them came over and pointed, first at my shampoo bottle, then at herself. The bottle was more empty than full, so I handed it to her. She unscrewed its top, smelled the contents then put a little drop of shampoo on her finger before dabbing it behind each ear, smiling with pleasure as she did so. I let her keep the bottle.

TOS Squadron deployed in Jebel Akhdar

The water in those falaj tanks, as soft as can be, was collected there by ancient channels that directed water down from the jebel. The actual tanks were cut from solid rock.

Very early one morning, I am woken up by the sound of machine gun fire. I grab my revolver from under my pillow and am about to wake my soundly sleeping colleagues when I realise there is no return fire. The sound seemed to be coming from some distance away, but was near enough to stir the blood. There was no alarm and no activity that I was aware of, so I went back to sleep, thinking that some poor sod must be in trouble.

It was 'stand to' time, and the fog was dense, so we listened more than saw. Suddenly, a stone was turned over in front of me. It was close. I crouched there and waited. A figure loomed out of the fog. A TOS uniform appeared. It was being worn by Colonel Carter. He drew level with me before I whispered,
'Good morning, sir.'
He was startled, but recovered quickly. 'Good morning, corporal. Is everything okay?'
'Yes, sir.'
'I've just come down to see that everything is all right,' the colonel said. 'I've been up on the mountain. Lucky for you, you were just out of range of that machine gun. The rebels didn't manage to bring it any further forward.

Another hundred yards, or so, and they could have strafed the whole camp. I suggest you laager up a bit more for your own protection.'

We did.

Inhospitable terrain in the region of Jebel Akhdar

We were on 'stand to' before dawn again. I could see the outline of a colleague on my right. He was signalling to me that he had heard something in front of him. We listened, but didn't hear anything. I moved over to him,

'I heard movement out there,' he breathed.

I listened intently. Then we both heard a faint noise about twenty yards in front of us. We separated and I issued a challenge, which was answered by,

'235_____ Trooper _____ SAS.'

I ordered him to come in.

When he appeared out of the mist, we asked him what he was doing, creeping in to our area. He told us that he had just lost his partner; shot and killed by a rebel sniper. The two SAS men had been trying to get into a sniping position, but the rebels already had it covered with their own sharp shooter.

'Come on, we'll put a brew on,' I told him.

Colonel Carter's voice came through the mist. 'It's okay, lads. I'll take care of him.'

I now had some idea what being in a shooting war was like. Hardly anyone involved knows what the hell is happening at any given moment.

Landmines found at Jebel

Sometime during my tour, I was requested by Bahrain to send them some highly classified documents. Examining aircraft manifests for the next few days, I discovered that only one TOS person was available to act as a courier, and that person was the MO. He was going on leave. As luck would have it, I met him the following day on his way to see the RAF Medical Officer.

'You are going on leave, sir.'

'Yes. I'm really looking forward to it.'

'Would you mind taking something through to Bahrain for me, sir?'

'No, I'm sorry, I can't. My plane arrives almost too late for me to get accommodation at the officers' club, as it is. He looked at me and sighed, 'I haven't got any option really, have I?'

'Not really, sir.'

'If you mess up my leave, corporal, I'll think of some way to get my own back!'

I met him at the aircraft steps and gave him the parcel which was fully strung and wax sealed. 'Keep hold of this, sir. If you go to the toilet it goes with you. Where ever you go, it goes.'

I received confirmation of the parcel's safe arrival - and all was well.

About two months later, I bumped into the MO again and asked if he had enjoyed his leave.

'It was very good, corporal.'

He then went on to describe his experience as a courier. 'When I got on the plane, clutching your damned parcel, I started planning your fate should I miss out on a room at the officers' club and be obliged to go and stay in some flea pit. As we came in to land at Bahrain, the pilot asked everyone to remain seated until they were told otherwise. There goes my room at the officers club, I thought. Some big wig is on the plane and will exit first. I looked out of the window and saw a military police Land Rover speeding over to our aircraft. Two MPs come on board and start walking up and down the aisle, looking at the passengers.

One of them stops at my side. 'Captain_____?'

'Yes.'

'You have a parcel?'

I tried to give it to them.

'No, sir, you keep that. Would you come with us, sir?'

I am escorted off the plane and seated in the back of the Land Rover. I ask them what's going to happen to my luggage. 'You will get that later on, sir.'

I am really cursing you by now, corporal. I have no chance of getting a room at the officers club. I've no luggage and don't know where I am going. We drive straight to some building in town, and I am taken up to the second floor. A young lieutenant turns up and asks me for the parcel, which I give him.

'I'll be on my way, then,' I say to him.

'Sorry, sir, but we need to check the contents of the parcel before you can go. Would you like a cup of tea while you are waiting?'

I finished my tea and the lieutenant returns. 'Everything appears to be in order, sir.'

As I get up to leave, he says, 'The two gentlemen who brought you here will take you to the officers' club, sir.'

The two MPs escorted me into the club's foyer and ask me to wait while one of them goes over to the reception desk. Upon his return, they both escort me up to a first floor room. An MP puts a key in the lock and the door opens. 'There you are, sir.' He hands me the key. I walk into the room and there is my luggage, and it's not just a room, it's a suite of rooms! All is forgiven, corporal. If you ever want a courier again, I'm your man!'

My tour with the TOS came to an end as the force was increasing in size. By then, my own position required two Royal Signals NCOs. I was not sorry to leave, just sad. The people I have known and those veterans I still know today, cannot be bettered.

TOS Patrol to Ibri

Motorway services, Trucial Oman style

3

THE FIVE-YEAR MAN

John Hopkins RA

On 9th April 1957, having completed recruit training with 24th (Irish) Battery, 17th Training Regiment RA at Park Hall Camp, Oswestry, Shropshire, and having had some leave, l left home for Liverpool Street Station. Mum and dad insisted on accompanying me. As the train departed for Harwich l'm sure l detected faint tears in mum's eyes. Personally, l was very happy as l was off on what l considered a great adventure at the start of my career as a Gunner Technical Assistant RA. As the train approached Harwich, I saw a very large sign which stated – 'Harwich for the Continent!' Some wag had graffitied below it, these words, 'And Frinton for the incontinent!

Along with some other Gunners, I boarded the Empire Wansbeck. As we did so, we were issued with a blanket and a pillow case. We were then herded below decks to a huge dormitory of bunk beds, four-tiers high, with, it seemed, only about eighteen inches clearance between each of them.

The ship set out on its overnight crossing of the North Sea, heading for the Hook of Holland; it was a very rough crossing. I can still remember the sounds made by packed soldiery heaving and spewing as the ship bounced its way across the Channel.

Upon arrival at the Hook, we were given a bread roll, filled with something or other, and a mug of tea, before being marched to the railway station where trains designated 'Red', 'Green' and 'Blue', waited to take their passengers to various destinations.

I boarded the train for Detmold and settled into my seat. This was only my second trip abroad. A Royal Signalman in our compartment was destined, as he insisted, for Hereford. We told him there was no chance of him getting there because he wasn't even in the right country! But he wouldn't listen. He was, of course, bound for Herford!

Eventually, the train drew into Detmold Hbf, where vehicles from our new regiment picked us up and delivered us to Hobart Barracks, which had been built by the Wehrmacht in the 1930s. For the foreseeable future, I would be serving with 10th Self-Propelled Regiment RA, (soon to become 10th Field Regiment RA). The regiment was armed with 25-pounder howitzers, mounted in tracked Sextons. We also had some tracked Priest vehicles, armed with 105mm guns. The regiment had served in the Western Desert during 1942 and took part in the D-Day landings, after which they fought their way across Europe until they arrived in the Detmold area in May 1945. There they had stayed. Later, during 1957, the regiment was under orders to proceed to Piddlehinton Camp in Dorset. Erected in 1940, its last occupants had been Americans, based there prior to D-Day!

The Commanding Officer, Adjutant, Quartermaster and RSM made a reconnaissance trip to Piddlehinton and came back to Detmold, seething with rage. The CO, feeling that the camp was unworthy of a regiment that had fought an honourable war, decided to refuse to move! At this time, 19th Field Regiment, stationed in Hong Kong, was earmarked to be put into suspended animation. Finally, the War Office decided that our regiment would be 'mothballed' instead. 19th Regiment would be sent to Germany. This happened in December 1957.

I was posted to St George's Barracks, Minden, with about one hundred other personnel of 10th Regiment, to await the arrival, in dribs and drabs, of 19th Field Regiment. By the end of 1959, I had slipped into the post of Battery Clerk and had a new qualification - Clerk Class III. I could see that my future years with the regiment would be the same as the previous two. Now a bombardier, I wanted a change of scenery and found the opportunity to have it when I was browsing in the Garrison Library. I discovered a couple of pamphlets advertising the virtues of service on secondment with the Jamaican Defence Force and the Trucial Oman Scouts. The latter pamphlet asking the question, 'Are you the man?' I decided to volunteer for service with both units.

Before long, I had been provisionally accepted by the Trucial Oman Scouts. The only bug-bear was that they would not accept me until I upgraded my clerical qualifications. A signal was sent off to Woolwich, requesting they enrol me on a Class II course.

I actually emerged from Woolwich with a Class 1 Trade qualification and, in July 1960, found myself on the way to join the legendary Trucial Oman Scouts.

I went there via Brize Norton, Cyprus and Bahrain.

Upon arrival at Muharraq Airport, Bahrain, the RAF Warrant Officer Loadmaster informed us passengers that the order of disembarkation would be, senior officers first, followed by families and other officers, then the rest of us. He then called 'Brigadier Hopkins' forward.

No-one moved, so he called the name again, repeating it a couple of times. I decided to move down the aisle to the Loadmaster. A look of puzzlement crossed his face when he was confronted by a soldier, aged twenty one. I informed him that I was Bombardier ('Bdr' on the passenger list) Hopkins. His look changed to one of anger and embarrassment. Speaking in a whisper, he told me to disembark and not tell a b***** soul what had happened!

The Sheikh of Sharjah's Palace

After kicking my heels in Bahrain for a while, I was eventually allocated a seat on a Gulf Air flight to Sharjah.

I was met off the 'plane by a TOS corporal named Sanderson. He was acting as post orderly. By an extraordinary coincidence, when we stopped off at the RAF Post Room to pick up some mail, there, crouching on the floor and wearing a Trucial Oman Scouts' uniform, was Captain Guy Hoad from 10th Field Regiment. I walked up behind him and said something along the lines of, 'Good morning, sir. This is a bit of a change from Detmold.'

I learned that Captain Hoad and his good friend from those days, Lieutenant Peter Postlethwaite were employed as Desert Intelligence Officers! Their duties obliged them to travel throughout the entire Trucial States in Land Rovers, with an Arab crew. Dressed in 'civilian' clothes, they looked more like tramps or pirates, than British army officers. Their tasks included visiting sheikhs, emirs, walis (tribal leaders) and other notables, gathering local intelligence on such things as strangers visiting the area, rumours of gun runners and illegal immigrants, ascertaining tribal loyalties, reporting on crop harvests and the condition of the water at various wells and oases.

Initially, I was employed in the Force Headquarters in 'G' Branch, which was a fascinating place to work. Very early one morning, I was due to relieve the overnight duty clerk. Slipping my foot into one of the leather sandals that were standard issue, I saw that there was a very large camel spider in the other. The monstrous creature, I mean it was as big as a dinner plate, had four legs inside the sandal and the other four outside!

My heart missed a couple of beats before the spider was sent to wherever spiders go, by the only weapon available - a collapsible chair!

I can remember going with a small party of soldiers and an officer on a journey from Sharjah Camp to deliver a 25-pounder field howitzer and a stock of blank cartridges to Sheikh Rashid bin Humaid al Nuaimi of Ajman. It seemed that the Foreign Office had considered this 'saluting cannon' to be a suitable gift! The sheikh's only question was, 'If it fired real shells, would they reach Sharjah from here? I think he was joking, on the other hand, he was the spitting image of the warrior, Auda abu Tayi in 'Lawrence of Arabia', so who knows? He kindly provided us with a very tasty fadhl (feast), consisting of curried goat and rice. This was the first and last time I tried eating a goat's eyeball!

Camel Spider

Christmas 1960 came, and I volunteered to act as postman for the outlying Squadrons, (or, in my mind, Santa!). A Bedford truck, with an Arab driver, took me on a three day tour to all four of them, including Manama Recruit Depot. It was a fascinating and interesting trip for me, as I was usually confined to Force Headquarters. After all these years I can still remember having breakfast with B Squadron's commander. He seemed to live on a diet of curried goat and brandy!

Another memorable commander was Major Meredith Budd MBE, a fellow-artilleryman, he had been with the Scouts since 1955, and by the time I departed in November 1965, he had served in every officer-post, apart from Commander Trucial Oman Scouts. He eventually retired to Andorra.

During my first leave, my mother was adamant that she wanted a photograph of me in the Scouts' uniform. She duly made an appointment with a local photographer. I arrived at the studio wearing civilian shirt and jeans and carrying a case. I told the photographer that I wished to put on my uniform. He directed me to go behind a screen. When I emerged wearing my TOS blue shirt, shemagh and aghul, his face was, if you will excuse the pun, a real picture, but not once did he question me!

Corporal Dave Youell, of the 17/21 Lancers, went on a lone trip up country without conforming to Standard Operating Procedures, i.e. booking out and warning those at his destination that he was on his way. True to form, his Land Rover broke down in the desert. He only survived by drinking the contents of the radiator. It was a warning to us all. Some rules were worth sticking to.

Sheikh Rashid bin Humaid al Nuaiimi of Ajman

During 1961, our well-loved and respected commander, Colonel Stewart Carter OBE MC, ex-Sherwood Foresters, left the Trucial Oman Scouts. His replacement was Colonel Hugh Bartholomew OBE, ex-King's Own Border Regiment.

Colonel Carter could sometimes give the impression that he was absent-minded. An example of this was when I was detailed to act as escort to a British soldier charged with causing a traffic accident. The RSM marched the accused and escort into the colonel's office. He was sitting at his desk, perusing some papers. After the Adjutant had read out the charge, Colonel Carter looked me in the eyes, and said,

'Well, what have you got to say for yourself?'

The RSM said, 'He's the escort, sir!'

A Scottish officer, let's call him Major McGonigle, went to the UK on compassionate leave in order to visit his seriously ill father. Sadly, his father died. Upon his return, he informed me that he was now a clan chieftain and his name had become McGonigle of McGonigle, The Black McGonigle. I gave him my condolences on the death of his father and pointed out that on Part ll Orders he would have to remain as Major McGonigle, as we were restricted to seventeen letters for surnames. He told me not to be so stupid - but he remained Major McGonigle!

On 17th July 1961, while on an exercise, a Land Rover and a Bedford QL truck were involved in a head-on collision during the night. Under orders to 'show no lights', Lieutenant Aspinall RAMC and Lieutenant Rowarth RASC, and an Arab soldier in the Land Rover, were killed. Three Arab soldiers in the Bedford were also killed. A surviving Arab soldier described the collision as a land-mine explosion.

One day, my bearer, Ali, presented me with a beautiful peregrine falcon. I looked after it for a couple of days before I discovered that it was owned by Sheikh Saqr III bin Sultan al-Qasimi of Sharjah, and must be restored to him immediately. It was returned by Major Budd, a true gentleman who always had a friendly word to say to the British soldiers. He had had a most interesting career, having served with the Sudan Defence Force from 1945 to 1950, the 1st Singapore Regiment from 1950 to 1953 and The Arab Legion from 1953 to 1955. He joined the Trucial Oman Scouts in 1955 and served with them until 1971, making him the longest continuous serving officer. I was lucky enough to be second to him in length of continuous service.

1961 Colonel Stewart Carter handing over to Colonel Hugh Bartholomew

One of the officers who joined the Scouts, arrived at his allotted Squadron and was promptly 'Returned to Unit' for attempting to spread Christianity by translating the Bible to his Arab soldiers!

The commander of 'X' Squadron was Major Ken Wilson of the Royal Scots. Rumour has it that, one evening, in an Officers' Mess in Bahrain, he got into conversation with the commanding officer of one of the Parachute Regiment's battalions exercising in the Gulf. The outcome was that Major Ken bet the para officer that his Squadron could run rings around his lot, out in the desert. The bet was duly accepted and eventually the paras dropped into the Trucial States. They set up camp and waited to be attacked by 'X' Squadron. After three or four days, their CO asked by radio when 'X' Squadron would be attacking. He was asked when the last water bowser had got through to them to deliver much needed supplies. It was only then that the para commander realised that 'X' Squadron didn't need to attack them; all they had to do was snaffle the paras' water and other supplies on their way up to them! Major Ken won his bet.

The Trucial Oman Scouts began to change as certain officers attempted to turn the force into a copy of their own battalions. I will always remember the Friday morning parade taken by the deputy commander. The unsmiling officer confined himself to announcing,
  'Ileum ana bafateesh parade Inglesi - barden Workshops.' (today I inspect the English, later the Workshops)
  Perhaps he didn't know the Arabic for rifle squadron, signals squadron or motor transport squadron!

During 1962, the new TOS Barracks were finished and we left the dilapidated communal huts for the so-called luxury of single, air-conditioned rooms. Instead of earthenware pots of water strategically placed outside our huts, we had permanent supplies of ice-cold, filtered water. The inside temperature of our new rooms was about 85F; outside summer temperatures being of the order of 130F. The result was that many of us went down with colds and the 'flu'!
  Sometime during the same year, I smashed my glasses and, needing a completely new pair, was flown to Aden. I was placed in the transit camp there. A sergeant-major said that I would be put on guard duty the following night. He also ordered me to get out of my 'funnies' and get into regular British Army uniform. I explained that the shemagh, aghul, blue shirt and khaki slacks were my uniform, and, anyway, I didn't possess a single item of British Army kit. A glazed look came over his face as he wandered away, muttering to himself, 'I don't know what the British Army's coming to.'

One morning, a signal was received from the Buraimi Squadron, stating that there had been a traffic accident involving a Bedford carrying 125 civilian passengers. I sent a reply asking them to confirm the numbers as I found it to be rather excessive. The answer came back, '125, repeat, 125!' Amazingly, no-one was killed in this incident, although the vehicle had overturned. In April 1963, an RAF Twin Pioneer crashed, killing three British servicemen and three Arab soldiers. At the RAF Board of Enquiry, the sole surviving Arab soldier was asked to describe the sequence of events. He stated that the engines began to misfire, there was a very loud crash and Allah's hand had plucked him from the wreckage and placed him on a sand dune!

Most afternoons, many of the British soldiers serving with the TOS, departed for the beach. We arrived there once, to find that the wreckage of an aircraft had been revealed by shifting sands. It was thought to be a Blenheim. This was never confirmed, though, because when the find was reported to RAF Persian Gulf, they showed no interest! Some of us indulged in various hobbies, including, at one time, a zoo, run by Corporal McFadyen! He had jerboas, desert foxes, various lizards and a pit viper!

Hawker- Hunter!

When a smallpox epidemic erupted within a large group of illegal immigrants from Baluchistan, an isolation camp was set up. WO2 Charlie Brown RAMC worked tirelessly within the camp to tend the sick. For his sterling work in a very perilous situation he was awarded the British Empire Medal.

The Scouts had a number of Arab horses stabled on a hill above Sharjah Camp. A sergeant of the Royal Horse Artillery was in charge of them. I suppose, to keep the Foreign Office 'on side', they were designated as patrol horses. As far as I was aware, they were never used for any patrolling. Instead, they provided sport for anyone who thought they could ride. Very reluctantly, many of the British soldiers were encouraged to take advantage of the chance to learn to ride at the Foreign Office's expense. Early one evening, I appeared at the stables, along with a few others. We were given the most rudimentary verbal instructions, after which, we mounted and set off, line astern, into the desert. My mount, a black Arab stallion named 'Shaitan' (Devil). Initially, Shaitan was quite well behaved, but, all of a sudden, he began snorting and picking up speed. After we had overtaken three or four of the other horses and their riders, Shaitan made a bee-line for an Arab mare and tried to mount her, knocking the mare's rider to the ground and dislodging me at the same time. It was the first and last time I took advantage of the Foreign Office's largesse!

One autumn, a convoy was being driven through a dry wadi bed when a sudden thunderstorm struck the area. The subsequent flood waters completely engulfed the vehicles, reducing some of them to scrap. Later, when the wreckage was recovered, two of the largest pieces were found to be the engine block and half the chassis of a Bedford. An Arab sergeant risked his life to save some soldiers from the flood and was later awarded the Military Medal for his bravery.

An RSM, who will not be forgotten by those who served with him, was WO1 (RSM) 'Tex' Mutter of the Royal Sussex Regiment. Our summer working hours were from 0600 hours to 1300 hours and RSM Mutter was usually the first in the Sergeants' Mess for lunch. On one occasion, he was ordering his dessert when the rest of the Mess members arrived in the dining room. He asked the Baluchi waiter what was on offer and was informed that it was apple crumble and custard. After a couple of minutes, the waiter reappeared and gave the RSM a bowl in which there was a black concoction covered in custard.

The RSM nearly had apoplexy and demanded to see the head chef. The chef, another Baluchi, duly appeared rubbing his hands with glee and grinning from ear to ear; expecting to be congratulated on the exquisite quality of his culinary delights. When the RSM demanded to know what was in the bowl, the chef told him it was apple crumble and custard. And where, Mutter enquired, did he get black apples from! The chef replied that, as he didn't have any apples, he had used prunes, but had religiously followed the recipe for apple crumble, ergo; what was in the bowl was apple crumble! Even RSM Mutter, had to splutter and hide a smile!

One of our lively Arab horses

Quite late in my service with the Scouts, we took a shotgun with us on a dhow trip to the Island of Abu Musa. In my early days with the force, Abu Musa had been unoccupied, apart from a small shack on a headland. That had been part of its charm. Now, soon after our arrival, we were visited by some villagers who, with difficulty, conveyed to us that their livestock was being depleted by a rather persistent eagle and could we, perhaps, do something about it? Corporal Stan Moult and I wandered off to see if we could find the culprit. We soon spotted the eagle sitting on some rocks, but as we got within shotgun range, it flew off and landed on a fence a couple of hundred yards distant. It continued to tantalize us by keeping just out of range as we moved in on it. After spending some hours trying to get near enough to the bird to shoot it, Stan and I had had enough. We decided to get back to our campsite. During our return journey, Stan suddenly spotted it, high in the sky. I took a bead on it and fired both barrels. For some time nothing seemed to happen, but all of a sudden Stan cried out,

'It's coming in like a 707!'

The eagle crashed to earth a few hundred yards from us and, upon inspection, was found to be dead. I felt absolutely rotten and ashamed, and have never killed an animal since.

Resolving a tribal dispute: Major Budd, Major Severn and Captain Ash sit with tribal elders and talk it through. This diplomatic approach earned the trust of the locals and prevented bloodshed.

In November 1965, I departed from Sharjah to begin six months' leave before joining the 45th Field Regiment RA at Shoeburyness, as Sergeant (Artillery Clerk), the Regimental Chief Clerk. The five years and four months' continuous service in the Gulf stood me in very good stead for the rest of my twenty-four years' service and I will never forget them, or those I served with.

At one of the earliest Trucial Oman Scouts' Association reunions, a group of us were standing together, chatting about old times. Some of those present hadn't seen each other for about a quarter of a century, so, in some cases, it was difficult to recognize each other. Someone asked, 'What was the name of that ___ ___ of a sergeant-major?' At once, a voice piped up, 'That was me!'

Major Ken Wilson 'X' Squadron

4

MODEL T FORD IN THE TOS

Tony Ford RAOC

Working in an orderly room, one gets sight of many interesting documents and it was through a Defence Council Instruction, whilst serving in Cyprus in the early autumn of 1957, that I was alerted to the need for volunteers to serve with the Trucial Oman Scouts. I had spent a year with 'O' Force in Aqaba, Jordan, and was interested in the mysteries of the Arab world. Without further ado, I signed on the dotted line, not knowing whether I was likely to be accepted. Within a month or so, I received a posting order and with all my worldly goods was driven from the Troodos Mountains to Nicosia. A Hastings aircraft brought me to Bahrain, and the weekly Valetta flight, to Sharjah. It was, I believe, November 7th 1957.

I was met by the Orderly Room Quartermaster Sergeant, Ken Tiley.

At my billet, early on this Tuesday morning, most of the occupants were still in bed.

Strange it was, until I learned that the working week did not include Tuesdays and Fridays. Later on, this arrangement was changed to Sundays off and, later still, to just Fridays, to conform to the Muslim day of prayer.

The following day, it was off to headquarters to report for duty; and to the Quartermasters' department to hand in the Sten gun and ammunition I had been issued with on the disbandment of the British garrison in Aqaba. I had carried it with me to Cyprus, and on to the Trucial Oman Scouts. I mention this because, almost five years later, I was called up to see the Quartermaster of 7th Armoured Brigade to account for the weapon that had been issued to me four and a half years earlier. I was required to state, in writing, that I had handed it in. Later on, I visited Hameln, where one of the storekeepers, Corporal Parsons, who had served with the Scouts, was stationed, and asked him about the 'missing' weapon.

'Oh,' he said, 'we were carrying out an arms check as part of the War Office annual controlled stores census and found we were a weapon in hand. We thought it best to get rid of it quietly, so we took it into the desert and blew it up!'

I worked mainly in the orderly room with three Indian clerks, Mr Nair, Mr Chaudary, and Mr Menon, looking after the British officers and NCOs records, as well as the classified documents we held. I was also Travel and Post NCO and was consequently issued with a Land Rover for this purpose - although I had never taken driving lessons and didn't hold a driving permit! Nobody asked me to sign for the Land Rover, either! With this vehicle, I went to Dubai twice a week to pick up mail, mainly for Indian staff, although there were also letters for Arab soldiers, mainly from Dhofar. When I eventually handed the Land Rover back, I was told that the spare wheel was missing and the chassis was cracked. Not knowing that signing for a vehicle was the norm, I pleaded innocence. Fortunately, the Land Rover was sold locally and the affair quietly forgotten. I had only re-mustered as a clerk a year before, so I didn't really know how to solve many of the problems I faced.

Within a couple of weeks of my arrival, the ORQMS left me in charge while he went off to Aden for rest and recuperation and to buy the Christmas draw prizes for the Sergeants' Mess. Upon his return to Sharjah, I was given a dressing down by the second in command, Major Pott, for slacking. He warned me that if there was no improvement in my work, I would be kicked out. In my defence I said that I had only been a clerk for a year and it was unfair that, as a private soldier, my qualities should be judged against those of a warrant officer. Within three weeks I was told to get a tailor's chit and have one stripe sewn on my shirts. Two weeks after that, I was told to promulgate the order promoting me to corporal. It's a funny old world.

It was normal procedure to work each day until about one o'clock and then have the remainder off. Sometimes I would be obliged to work after lunch, and on one of these occasions, the force commander, Colonel Carter, came into my office.

We had a field telephone system that operated through a switchboard in the Signals Centre. Colonel Carter wanted to make a call and used the telephone on my desk to do so. When he got through, the voice at the other end said,

'City Desk, Al Capone speaking.'

'Ah, Al Capone,' Colonel Carter replied, 'I've always wanted to meet you, would you like to come down to HQ and step into my office?'

Colour Sergeant "Jigger" Lee had 'acquired' a donkey which roamed about the camp in Sharjah. It would respond to a whistled call. Those in the know would only whistle when close to a building where refuge could be sought, otherwise the donkey would become frisky and attempt to mount the whistler. Some of the airmen on camp did not appreciate the animal's amorous advances. In due course, the senior RAF officer, who was nominally also Garrison Commander, sent a three or four page letter outlining reasons, such as safety, hygiene, etc, why the donkey should be disposed of. Colonel Carter's reply was just one word – 'No.'

TOS soldier with Jebel Akhdar in the background

During 1958 and 1959, the British element of the Scouts expanded. When I first arrived, there were no more than twenty corporals; when I left, there were about sixty. In fact, expansion was so rapid that not enough volunteers from the Pay Corpsc could be found from the Regular Army, so a number of National Servicemen were asked if they would like to do a stint with the TOS. Those that did, fitted right in

The increase in the British element had its good points as well as its bad. We were now confronted with having a British sergeant major in Headquarters Company, and we all know that Sergeant Majors look for work, not for themselves - for their subordinates. And so it was in Sharjah.

It was deemed that we should train for war – well, at least train for civil unrest and disorder. We would 'get on' parade in the afternoons and train for riot control, forming open squares and marching through the camp with the sergeant major shouting at the non-existent crowd we were supposed to be controlling. He would bellow the order,

'Take aim at the man with a red bobble hat!' Followed by, 'Third man on the right from centre; shoot!'

Mine was the easy task. I was the recorder of the proceedings, sitting in a Land Rover with watch, pen, and pencil. These drills did manage to instil a certain amount of discipline into those who took part in them.

Cpl "Mafeesh teeth" Wilkinson

We went out on armed watch. Leaving at dusk in a Land Rover; armed with a rifle and a radio set, we followed the coastal road. In order not to draw attention to anyone in the area, we would jump off the moving vehicle, one by one, and lay in wait for camel trains suspected to be running arms. We would spend the entire night keeping a look out for them, but never had any luck. The gun runners, although at that time they were more likely to be smuggling mines, probably landed miles away, on the Batinah coast. These night forays did add a bit of spice to life, though.

It was dirty work repairing vehicles, and there was always plenty of dust to contend with. Once or twice a week we travelled down the wadi that led from Hijar to the falaj near Awabi. There we could bathe in fast flowing water coming down from the surrounding mountains. Since it was used for irrigating the gardens of Awabi, we could only use soap sparingly. An SAS unit visited us again in late 1959. They set up their rear command post next to our barrack block, so we maintained close contact with them and sank the odd beer or two together.

Some time after this, there was a large joint exercise, involving an aircraft carrier, the Royal Marines, armoured vehicles, the Muscat Regiment and the Scouts - on the Batinah coast, inland from Sohar. I went on this escapade, and when we paraded on the second day, having reached the coast, the convoy commander asked if anyone could act as a guide.

One of the jobs I undertook at the end of 1958 was to build the Christmas bar in the signals block. At this stage, there were about forty corporals. We were divided into two barrack blocks - however, two days before Christmas; 'Mafeesh (no) Teeth' Wilkinson, another vehicle mechanic, and I, were sent up country with the SAS for the first serious advance on the rebel stronghold situated on Jebel Akhdar. Most of my time on this operation was spent in helping to repair vehicles. Our hardest task was replacing a gearbox on a water bowser. We only had one jack and a dozen or so helping hands to push the vehicle away from the engine and gearbox when they were removed. Dismantling them was a fairly simple task. We held the engine unit steady on the jack, as the vehicle itself was allowed to roll slowly down an incline. Re-fitting the engine to the truck required the vehicle to be pushed back up the incline. The job had to be completed in a day or so because the bowser was the only source of water for the camp. Another task was replacing the cab on a three ton winch vehicle – the replacement came from a mined lorry that had been left in the Muscat Armed Forces scrap yard.

I had already spent three months in the area and knew about the subkha problems, where wadis ran into the sea. After the exercise had been completed and we were on our way back to Sharjah, five trucks became bogged down at a point where a subterranean river ran out to a beach. The only means of extricating them was to bring a Scammel recovery vehicle out from Sharjah. After five tides had washed over the trapped vehicles, we loaded their contents on to other lorries and continued our journey. We met the Scammel while we on the way home to Sharjah. Needless to say, the abandoned trucks were all write-offs.

The perils of the coastal subkha

In early 1960, there was another exercise in the Ibri, Nizwa, Izki area, and a large force of Scouts took part. I travelled with the recovery vehicle - I can't remember who was with me. While passing Ibri, the medical officer's Land Rover was blown up by a mine. Three Scouts in the same vehicle suffered from shock and internal injuries. We did what we could to help them, but because the MO was there, we were somewhat superfluous.

As ours was the last vehicle in the convoy, we raced on to catch up with the others and 'sound the alarm'. The convoy commander didn't want to stop. It was only when I protested that the three casualties no longer had any transport and that at least parts of the mined vehicle and its contents needed to be recovered (radio, medicines, personal equipment, etc) that anyone was sent back. We heard later that the Sultan's Armed Forces imposed their will on the local villagers by blowing up houses and fining the inhabitants. The exercise was mainly a show of strength, with the Sultan's air force firing rockets from Jet Provosts.

In August 1960, the Desert Regiment was formed, and I went to Buraimi with Dave Orme, John Beckett, Jock Mathieson, Charlie Allen and the medical orderly, Staff Sergeant Finch. We were there for a month before someone realised that the Trucial Oman Scouts here presence was not in accord with a United Nations agreement that troop levels in the oasis should not be increased while the on-going dispute with Saudi Arabia remained unresolved. For that short period of time, the Desert Regiment was based in Beyt Aquil, which I believe is in the Omani sector of the oasis.

Colonel Carter, the Commander of the Scouts, paid us a visit. He was spending the night at Beyt Aquil and I was responsible for catering for the small British contingent. Knowing that the colonel planned to visit 'A' Squadron at Fort Jahili, I asked him whether he would be staying with Major Budd for dinner or would he be coming back to us that evening.

'I'm coming back here,' he said. 'I couldn't stand being fed on ants' balls in aspic!'

Major Budd was known for his unusual palate, his desires being met by deliveries from Fortnum and Mason.

Ibri Camp

After three weeks, we packed our bags once again and moved to Idthen, near Dhaid, but not without a minor disaster. Due to the dust being kicked up by the vehicles in front of him, one of the Bedford truck drivers failed to see that the convoy had stopped. As a result, thirteen trucks shunted into each other after he ran into the back of a stationary lorry. The driver escaped with a broken leg.

In Idhen (now spelt Adhan, I believe) I remained responsible for the catering arrangements for the sergeants and corporals, although we did have a locally enlisted cook, and a Baluchi waiter, whom we named, Caruthers. To relieve the monotony of living on biscuits or unleavened bread, I set to and built a baking oven out of an oil drum and a flimsy fuel can. The oven was heated by means of a Primus stove. I would make bread twice a week, taking half a day to bake two loaves. They would be taken out of the oven during early afternoon so that they were ready to eat with the evening meal. All went well for the first two or three sessions, then, after being left to cool, they would disappear. At first I thought the culprit was the cook or waiter. No amount of questioning could reveal the name of the light fingered culprit. Eventually, in a bid to find out who it was, I hid behind our mess tent and peered through the openings between the wall and the roof. I caught him bread-handed!

I went to Sharjah in March to undergo my next, pre-tour, medical. When the Medical Officer (who had been suitably primed by the Parachute Regiment records officer) asked how long I had been with the TOS - three and a half years at the time; he asked,
'And where were you before you came here, Germany?'
'No, sir,' I replied, 'Cyprus.'
'And before that?'
'Jordan, sir.'
I had been in the Middle East for almost five years - hence I was put on the next plane out. And so ended my tour with what, for me, had been the formative and best years of my life. I was a private soldier when I had been put in charge of the TOS Records Office. By the time I left the Scouts, there were two officers and a number of NCOs all working on pay and records, a far cry from the situation in 1957.

That is a potted history of my time with an elite force, but in amongst all this, there are other memories, including - the movement of the Pay Office to its new location, adjacent to our headquarters. All went well until it came to moving the paymaster's safe. By this time, the workshop had a crane, and having removed the roof of the pay office and lifted the safe out to transport it to its new location, we literally hit a snag. It had almost reached the end of its short journey when the cable suspending the safe encountered a high tension cable. With a bang and a flash it plummeted to the ground - the cable having been severed by the electric current. I also recall the antics we TOS corporals got up to at the open-air cinema; generally showing our disapproval of the films and the long waits when reels had to be changed. One time, the Medical Officer had all the British staff assembled there in order to lecture us on the evils of going out with the prostitutes in Dubai and Sharjah. He brought in a lad of about sixteen years of age, riddled with syphilis, saying he had only about six months to live - he worked in the Dhobi shop; the laundry.
One last anecdote. It was one of those three-day Muslim holidays and in order to provide the British corporals with something to do, a road building party was put together to start creating a pass through the mountains to Dibba.

We set off, and after passing Idhen, turned inland along a broad wadi and then into a much smaller one, until we could go no further. We set up camp and surveyed the area where the road building was to take place. The first thing that had to be done was levelling out the sides of the wadi to make it passable for a Land Rover. We set to work, shovelling scree and placing beehive charges to clear the more stubborn places. Before the charges were set, sentries were posted to ensure no one came near the area. I was sent to watch the westerly approach, and lo and behold, a camel driver with his three camels came into view. Much to his annoyance, I stopped him from going on until the explosives had done their work. We went back to shovelling scree, working our way down the slope, only to be stopped ourselves- by someone firing at us! After beating a hasty retreat, we got our weapons into place and stood by, ready to defend ourselves. The Arab driver we had with us was sent to try and ascertain who had done the shooting. It was the camel driver. He was also one of the sheikh's bodyguards. We agreed to stop our road building project. The work was being carried out at the local Sheikh's request, so one can only assume that he had not taken the precautionary step of informing his guards!

Cpl Tony Ford in Shariah

5

ITCHY FEET CAN TAKE YOU PLACES

Sid Falla Royal Signals

It is 1960 and I'm getting itchy feet again. I joined the army as a three-year regular in 1954 to avoid National Service and to get my choice of who I would serve with and where. As someone who fiddled around, building radios, the natural place for me to go was into the Royal Signals. The idea of communicating with people over vast distances fascinated me, and I felt a need to learn more about how it was done. So I elected to train as a radio operator. Basic recruit training at Catterick Camp in winter was not an experience designed to introduce us into a gentle or soft way of life. It was a tough wake-up call, and a rather brutal introduction to the army. Much was printed in the national press at that time about the appalling living conditions for recruits at Catterick Camp; they reported that horrific bullying by NCO instructors was a common occurrence. As new, raw recruits, most of us just accepted that it was part of the training and we were expected to learn how to live in less than favourable conditions. Looking back on it, I realised they had taken me in, shook me about and, at the end of recruit training, churned out another disciplined man. Next please!

Without exception, everyone was happy to leave basic training behind and move on to learning one's chosen trade.

My move was to Aines Lines, still at Catterick, but in an entirely different set up. This was the radio operator training school and I fell into it with enthusiasm, being there was, after all, my reason for joining.

It was like being back at school; life was regulated by time tables and a set daily programme.

We started Morse code training on day one. It was a relentless development, with tests every morning to assess progress. About a month into the course, we began to take formal Morse, receive and send tests. They used a tape recorder to transmit a simple five letter code at slow speeds, gradually building up the receiving speeds so that we were always chasing it. Sending Morse code is a lot more difficult than it looks and requires a great deal of practice to achieve a good 'hand' and rhythm. We were taught a whole lot of associated subjects so that we could go anywhere and had the skills to make a radio work.

I duly passed out as a fully-fledged radio operator, ready, able and enthusiastic enough to conquer the world of communications. They posted me to Malta Barracks in Aldershot.

RAF Handley Page Hastings

I had just ignored the first lesson of survival as a soldier; I had volunteered! This time it was for parachute training. Malta Barracks was home to 16 Parachute Brigade, Signal Squadron. It was where one prepared for 'pre-para' training. The powers that be would only allow those who were deemed 'suitable' to go forward to P Company, at Maida Lines in Aldershot, for yet another Selection process.

By any standards, P Company was tough! I now saw the benefit of recruit training. It had prepared me for a unit like that. My personal observations and experience led me to believe that the selection process was designed to take each individual, work them to their physical and mental limit and then go a step beyond. We could give up at any time; indeed, having been taken to the point of exhaustion, one of the instructors might tell you to give up because you were wasting everyone else's time.

The system worked, some succumbed and that was the end of their ambition to leap out of perfectly serviceable aircraft and earn half a crown (12.5p) per day, parachutist pay.

Paratroops inside a Hastings

Every hindrance to success was used; those instructors were masters at the art of making life difficult. It's also fair to say that they were with us every inch of the way, and whilst we thought we were fit, they were supremely so.

On the last day of the course, we were herded into the camp cinema to be given the news, pass or fail! For those who had managed to get this far, the success rate was usually less than twenty five per cent. From there, it was on to RAF Abingdon to begin ground training and preparations for the first of two jumps from a tethered balloon. After that little experience, it was on to exiting from a Hastings, four engine prop aircraft.

One night jump was included in the course. My memories of that included watching masses of sparks being ejected from the engines and flying past the door. We were told that, 'It's not easy to see the ground as you're falling towards it, so don't try to land before you hit it….!!' Very encouraging. It was an odd experience and I'm glad it was completed without injury.

One other incident gave me some mental anguish. We were doing a short three-stick exit from both sides of a Hastings, when the man immediately in front of me, refused to jump. He gripped the sides of the door and the dispatcher was unable to move him. Eventually when the green light went out and the red light came on he relaxed and the dispatcher took him to the back of the aircraft and sat him down. This left me in the joyful position of standing in the open door whilst we went around the circuit again and began a new approach. My mind was in a whirl, would I go or would I refuse? It was, however, a great way to enjoy a unique view of the Oxfordshire countryside, far below. I jumped.

Suez Canal blocked and Para dropping in on Port Said

After the 'Wings Parade', during which we were presented with our hard-won red berets and winged parachute badge, I returned to Malta Barracks in Aldershot. From there, I was posted to Barton Stacey. My first 'working unit' was the Signal Troop of the Airborne Gunner Regiment. To be honest, I thought I'd been shuffled off to the middle of nowhere. With precious little to keep me busy, I quickly realised that self-motivation was a necessary quality if one wanted to maintain and improve trade skills and fitness levels. I took every opportunity to build on all I had learnt so far. Not long after joining the regiment, it moved from C camp in Barton Stacy to North Camp in Aldershot.

It was now 1956 and President Nasser of Egypt was upsetting the British and French governments over the Suez Canal. In June, I was called back from leave and a few days later found myself on the aircraft carrier HMS Theseus, heading for Cyprus. It was not a holiday cruise; the smell of diesel was freely available to everyone all over the ship and was decidedly unpleasant. Glad I'm not a sailor. During the passage to Cyprus, we were worked very hard at fitness and weapon training. We also had lectures about medical matters, the history of the canal and associated British interests. Included in the weapon training were sessions of firing our personal weapons, mine was a Sten sub machine gun, at targets bobbing about on the sea behind the ship. Near the end of the voyage, we sailed through a storm where the waves were coming over the flight deck, so much for the calm waters of the Mediterranean! Six days after leaving the UK, we arrived at Famagusta on the south coast of Cyprus. From there, we were packed off to a temporary camp, and a couple of days later, moved on to a better one, set up by the Royal Engineers close to Nicosia Airport. EOKA terrorists kept us busy and we spent most of our time in the lovely Cyprus countryside and the Troodos Mountains, hunting for General Grivas and his followers. We really couldn't understand why the Greeks and Turks were at each other's throats but the whole experience in Cyprus was excellent training for our move to Egypt in November 1956. We were told that the aim of our trip to Egypt was to free up the Suez Canal, and in that we failed. As the CO's radio operator I was on the Brigade Radio network with direct access to Brigade HQ, which was set up in Port Said.

We were billeted in the Brooke Bond Tea factory. Early on, I remember that we were rushed out and set off south from Port Said on the road between Suez and the Sweet Water Canal, heading towards El Cap.

I was in my usual place in the back of the vehicle, looking after communications.

A little time after setting off, I received a message in Morse that said the cease fire was effective. I had no idea what they were talking about and couldn't believe it, so I asked for verification. They were clearly unprepared for such a request because it took some time for them to send the verification. When it did arrive, it satisfied me as being a genuine message, so I passed it on to the CO. He was not as surprised as I had been; it seemed that I was too low in the food chain to be briefed on such matters. It soon became apparent that politics had taken over. The Americans had told our government to stop whatever it was we were doing. By not being in the know, I effectively delayed the cease fire information by about an hour. So that was that. What a waste of effort.

That simple experience taught me to never keep my soldiers in the dark about what was going on, unless it was unavoidable.

We arrived back to a very foggy Southampton on an old liner called Ascania, a very efficient military movements organisation provided us with travel warrants and pay packets to get us home on Christmas Eve. After my tour with the para brigade, I decided to move back into the mainstream army in order to gain wider experience. After three good years with 19 Brigade Signal Squadron, I started to consider my position - and that brings me to 1960, the time when I wanted to try something new.

Part one daily orders quite often asked for volunteers for various postings and I saw one for secondment to an Arab force called The Trucial Oman Scouts. I tried to find out a bit more about them, but most people had no idea where the Trucial Oman Scouts were located, never mind what they did; but all were united in the opinion that it was likely to be a hot, sandy place. My career so far had prepared me for most things, but I still had no experience of desert soldiering. Give it a go, I said to myself, so, without having much idea of what it was all about or what it was I was getting myself into, I volunteered yet again. This turned out to be one of my better decisions. In 1961, I was sent to a place called Sharjah in the Trucial States, which, I discovered, was situated at the toe of Arabia. They gave me a posting order, a rail warrant to get me to London Heathrow, and a flight ticket to Bahrain.

The civilian Britannia, four engine turbo prop, buzzed its way to Istanbul, where it took on more fuel. This allowed us to leave the aircraft for a breath of fresh Turkish air and stretch our legs. My first taste of Turkish coffee left me with an opinion that was less than favourable, so orange juice was substituted, and that was good. After a couple of hours on the ground, we took off on the second leg to Bahrain. The aircraft landed at Manama in the middle of the night. As we left its cool interior, we walked into a wall of heat. It was only early May, but hot enough. The terminal buildings were very primitive, reminding me of a scene in the Humphrey Bogart film, 'Casablanca'.

There was an RAF Movements detachment on the airfield and I was directed to their office. The man on duty sent me to a transit hut and told me to report back the next morning, which I did. After a welter of explanations and to-ing and fro-ing, the RAF staff took me to a Twin Pioneer aircraft and introduced me to the flight crew. This is all a bit casual, I thought, where's all the red tape? That was it; we were off to Sharjah.

Arrival was pretty simple too; all I had to do was fill in the inevitable form. Another helpful RAF Movements chap whistled up a Trucial Oman Scouts vehicle and driver who delivered me to their HQ building on the outskirts of the airfield. I was expected, but no one seemed to know when I might turn up. After going through the usual procedures, I was taken to the billet that housed the TOS Royal Signals personnel. As I walked through the door, one of the guys who came to greet me, observed that I had also been greeted by a bed bug, a fat one was sitting on my shirt front. His cry to me not to squash it came a moment too late and the resultant large red stain never did completely wash out.

The following day I was taken to the QM stores to be issued with my Scouts uniform: shemagh and aghul, blue musree shirt, some shoulder badges, a red stable belt and lanyard, some lightweight trousers and a pair of the world's worst sandals. The leather was rock hard and some found them positively painful to wear. On day one, I discovered that there was much to learn and some things had to be learnt quickly. We were in a Muslim country and we needed to know the common courtesies; what to do and what not to do. Without some guidelines, one could unintentionally cause offence.

Bright and early on day two, I reported to the Signal Squadron and was interviewed by the Squadron Commander, Major Alistair McKinnon, who gave me a good briefing on the basic organisation of the Scouts, the outstation locations and the communication system. He went on to tell me that I was going to be NCO i/c the Signals Centre, staffed mainly by Arab radio operators. A round the clock radio network was established to the outstations at Manama, Fort Jahili at Buraimi, Mirfa, Masafi, Ras al Khaimah, Khor Fakkan and other locations such as Nizwa and Ibri, as necessary. The prime means of communicating was by Morse, but we did have a one hour voice schedule every morning for briefings and updates. The Desert Intelligence Officers could join in at any time. A separate, one to one, communications link was scheduled every morning with HQ British Forces in Bahrain, but we could join it whenever it was considered necessary. Occasionally, when Royal Navy ships were in the area, we were required to establish a radio link to them. These 'live' links were our only electronic means of communication within our own force and the outside world. There were no public telephone systems anywhere in the country.+ The Arab staff were extremely skilled and reliable Morse operators. Mostly, they didn't have good English reading skills, but that was irrelevant because they sent the correct code for each letter and recorded the correct letter for whatever they received back. The shape of the letters they had written down were sometimes difficult to work out, so I conducted individual training sessions designed to improve their writing skills. It was very rewarding, observing these young people developing and demonstrating their potential for the future.

All the main radio equipment operated on the HF band. To get the best from it, we relied heavily on the skills of the British operators to produce and erect the correct aerials for the various frequencies being used. For technical reasons, it is normal practice to change the frequency to suit the time of day or night. Each time a transmitter frequency was changed, a British operator and, when available, an Arab operator, would walk the two hundred yards to the site to effect the changes to both frequencies and aerials. The transmitter used to communicate with British Forces in Bahrain was an ancient and temperamental 53 set, a museum piece even then. The C12 radio set was a standard piece of equipment used on the operational net. We also owned, but in my time never used, an old Canadian 19 set (I knew how to use them, having been trained on them at Catterick). All our HF radios were free tuning, so accurate frequency settings were approximate. It was a problem we just had to live with. Alan Dicker, Nobby Lowe and a few others, set up an amateur radio station in a self-built shack adjoining the Signals Centre, with the call sign, MP4TAC.

Corporal Sid Falla

Most of the work had been done before I arrived, but I did get involved in building the cubical quad antennae and was nominated, as a qualified parachutist, to sit on top of the crane and guide it into place on top of a wooden pylon. I used the same call sign to work many stations around the world but ran into trouble when the force security officer called me to his office to explain why I, as NCO i/c the Signals Centre, was receiving lots of postcards from Box 88, Moscow!
'Ah, that was easy to explain, the Russians were getting a weak signal from the back lobe of the cubical quad and as a result they sent a QSL card to confirm a contact! Of course it never happened, no one would dream of acknowledging or reply to a Russian contact. Thank goodness he believed me!

The cubical quad antennae

The climate was red hot in the summer, but comfortable enough in the winter, and although we never had frost or snow, it was relatively cold at night, so warmer clothing was required. The humidity level along the coastal strip was often very high, causing an odd effect. We sometimes woke up in the morning to find the camp was enveloped in thick fog or mist. Anything not under cover was saturated. Old D8 telephone cable was used as guy ropes for our aerial masts; the cable is quite strong and was used in preference to the Hessian or sisal-type ropes that were available to us. The make-up of the cable includes some strands of steel and copper wire. It was the steel strands that gave the cable its strength. Unfortunately, although we should have known that steel rusts; it took us some time to realise why the guy ropes were snapping every now and again. Occasionally, when the guy ropes failed, the support masts came down and the aerials were found lying on the sand. Almost unbelievably, even when that happened we were still able to communicate, albeit with a poor signal.

None of what we of the Western World regarded as the basic necessities of life were available to us. No made up, black top roads, no telephone boxes from where we could call home, no roadside petrol stations or cafes; just lots and lots of sand. Huge dunes of soft stuff, followed by flat plains with a bone jarring corrugated surface. Each vehicle travelled as a completely self-sufficient unit with its own spare water, fuels, oils and spares. After our first trip into the desert, each one of us returned a wiser man, cognisant of the fact that we couldn't afford to make mistakes. It was an experience to be savoured, but sometimes only after the event.
The high humidity at Sharjah exacerbated the effect of the heat in Summer. Up country, it was a dry heat and easier to live with. High temperatures? What does that mean?

In 1962 we established contact on the amateur radio band with an American oil exploration ship which had entered the gulf and was planning to call in to Dubai and take on supplies. The operator was a Brit and invited us on board for a party once they had docked. They entertained us very well indeed and after a few beers, we thought it would be a good idea to invite them to a cricket match in Sharjah camp, the following day. They accepted. Forget the lovely manicured, green turf of England, we had a flattish area of hard sand, just outside the airfield, and an old, coir matted wicket. The recorded airfield temperature whilst we were playing was fifty degrees centigrade. Of course it wasn't always so hot, but July and August frequently were. During my tour, we moved out of the bedbug ridden barracks on the old airfield camp, into newly-built living accommodation, just a short distance away.

Members of the archaeological expedition- Sid Fall is sporting yellow flip-flops

We all had a personal ration box which contained a primus stove, utensils, a couple of chaguls (canvas water carriers) and whatever rations we cared to stock up with for a few days in the desert. Once we left Sharjah, we had to be entirely self-sufficient, and that included managing our own water and provisions. The deal was that once we had booked out from Sharjah, we were paid an allowance for each day away. This self-catering arrangement meant we could be deployed into any area at a moment's notice.

Running the Signals Centre allowed me to work closely with Arab NCOs and radio operators. This gave me plenty of opportunity to learn about their way of life and their customs. As Muslims, they observed their religious obligations with great dedication, in fact our working practices were designed to fit in with their devotions.

I had a young Baluchi boy operator of indeterminate age. At a wild guess, I suppose he was ten to twelve years old. He had some English, but was not proficient in speaking the language. His

Morse code skills were superb; he could receive fast code and accurately write down every symbol sent to him, and send clear, rhythmical Morse, fast or slow. He could do all of this with either hand.

We had an open air cinema on the camp that showed popular old films again and again - and again, but was, nevertheless, usually well attended. Being there was more of a social event than a night out at the movies. Although few and far between, live shows, arranged by a forces entertainment organization, would pay us an occasional visit. By far the most memorable of these was the Tommy Cooper show.

The day to day social scene was largely self-generated. It was not possible to go to the local pub for a pint! Alcohol was not available outside the camp. The REME contingent built an annex to their barrack block and turned it into a bar. This sounds easy, but they had to go through the usual hoops to satisfy the powers that be that it would be a well-run establishment, with supervising officers, etc. etc. Alcohol was duty free and therefore very cheap, but oddly enough, I can't recall any problems caused by over-indulgence in alcohol. It was considered bad form to show drunkenness in front of Arabs, and as we were all volunteers, we conformed to the local standards of behaviour, at least in public.

Every evening, an old man would tour the accommodation areas carrying a tea urn on his back and dispense a jolly good mug of chai, and, if ordered in advance, he would also provide a steak sandwich. Goodness knows what sort of meat he served, but it was palatable. The cost was minimal and I suspect he probably earned more in tips than in charges.

The old world encounters the new

Occasionally, we would have a 'death to bed bugs' day. Beds would be taken outside into the sun and every nook and cranny inspected and treated with a flame gun to get rid of them. The action made us feel better, but it had little effect. A fresh battalion would parachute down from the roof during the night. We tried putting the legs of the beds into small tins full of paraffin, this was supposed to deter the bugs, but that too had little effect. It was a never ending battle that we failed to win until we moved to the new accommodation block where everything was pristine, oh joy!

During the Easter holiday of 1962, a bunch of us decided to go on an archaeological expedition
. One of our number (names escape me) had heard that the University of Aarhus, in Denmark, had previously sent people into the country to search for possible clues to a Chinese occupation in the distant past. Armed with a rough idea of where to go and what to look for, we set off. First stop was Buraimi, to refuel and take on fresh water; then it was out into the desert. I can't remember exactly which direction we took, but after crossing a range of jebel, we eventually found a site that looked right to us; an igloo shaped lump on a hill top.

After we had set up camp, a plan of action saw us attacking the aforesaid 'igloo'. It was decided to cut into the side, for no other reason than it seemed like a good idea and was the easiest way to begin.

The digging was conducted on the top of a hill under a cloudless sky. It was hard, hot work. After many hours of toil, the stone wall we were attacking, gave way. As we had no idea what to expect, the consensus of opinion was that we had hit pay dirt. This was probably a burial mound. Over very many years, fine sand had filtered through to fill what had originally been a hollow centre. At that stage we started to sieve the sand we dug out, to check it for - we hadn't a clue!

Time passes, and after another hard day's digging, we began to find shards of bone and then small artifacts: an arrow head with a designed split head, a ruby ring and other items that confirmed human habitation. I made a plan of the dig, showing where we found each item. All the material, together with my plan of the dig was deposited at the British Museum in London when I returned home at the end of my tour.

A radio truck deployed in the desert

Some-time later, I received a letter from the University of Aarhus thanking us for passing on our findings and confirmed that it was a most valuable addition to their research.

Each Squadron, generally operating from its own base, was mostly self-sufficient and could deal with whatever problem was likely to be encountered. So far, few of us had any experience of a full force exercise bringing all the Squadrons together as a co-coordinated fighting force, but that was about to change.

Bedford three-to truck on radio testing tour of the outstations

A plan was being considered to set up a force exercise with all Squadrons taking part and being deployed from barracks, but with the base stations continuing to operate as usual. During the early planning stage, I suggested that we try out and test the mechanics of operating not only the regular radio networks, but also the proposed additional deployed field force networks. The frequency allocations were meagre and there were benefits to be gained from testing simulated multiple radio nets. I put together a crew consisting of both British and Arab operators, and with a schedule set-up, we went on a radio testing tour of the country. The Bedford three ton truck was a remarkably reliable and excellent cross country vehicle. This particular one was to be our home for the next few weeks.

I felt privileged to be travelling the country in this manner. They say that problems come in threes, and so it happened to us. While on a journey from Mirfa to Buraimi, the Bedford fan belt snapped. That was not a problem because all good drivers, and we had a good driver, carried a spare. Ours promptly fitted a new one, and off we went. But not for long! After a couple of hours, the new fan belt snapped. Now we did have a problem. It was about then that one of our British operators began to show signs of heat exhaustion. This became my priority, so I ordered one of the operators to get on the radio, call Jahili, and get them to send a Medic – and a fan belt. My reckoning put us about two hours, or so, from Buraimi. The operator came back to me and said,'The **** radio doesn't work!'

I checked the set and thought the aerial tuning unit box might be the problem and could probably be fixed. The heat exhaustion casualty was showing signs of distress so I got on with it, and repaired the set. Now we could call Jahili, explain our situation, and seek some help. Eventually, a Land Rover arrived with a spare fan belt and a medic, who, after examining the casualty, considered the man was in need of proper medical treatment and asked that we call for air casevac.

This was done and an aircraft was waiting at Buraimi airstrip when the Land Rover carrying the patient arrived there. He was flown to Sharjah and made a good recovery.

I enjoyed many other adventures during my time with the TOS. The days I spent in what is now the United Arab Emirates were very special; the whole experience; the people, the desert, the heat, the living conditions, my job and simply being there, proved to be a most rewarding and formative part of my life. Itchy feet can certainly get you places. Volunteering for service in the Trucial Oman Scouts proved to be one of my better decisions.

6

A COOK'S TOUR

Terry Ward ACC

A naïve, nineteen, going on twenty years old lance-corporal, I stood at the rail of the Troopship Oxfordshire, crammed between others of my ilk. I was looking down at two pretty young waitresses from the Sweet Garden Restaurant in Kam Tin. They were waving a tearful goodbye to me from the crowded Kowloon Dock. We had been no more than friends during my few months in Hong Kong, but one of them, the petite, Lin, had ambitions to marry a British soldier and be whisked away to that wonderland, the western world. Sorry to disappoint you, Lin.

Multi-coloured streamers provided a last tenuous connection between the passengers and those ashore as the ship began to tremble and move. Being of a somewhat romantic nature, tears welled up in my eyes as the Royal Marine Band, immaculate in their white uniforms, saw us off with, 'We'll meet again, don't know where, don't know when-'. It was December 1960.

Born into the world of high Sussex hedgerows and sunken lanes, I had become fascinated with big horizons, harsh desert landscapes and rugged jebel, while serving with 1st Field Battery (The

Blazers) in the Aden Protectorate, where I had lost two field kitchens, one from an explosion and one from a fierce sand storm, had a narrow escape from a flash flood, and learnt that, in a small outfit like ours, even a cook-corporal was expected to 'Stand to' with the gunners and return small arms fire when dissident tribesmen took pot-shots at us. 'STAND TO!' now there's an order that gets the adrenaline flowing! I'd seen death close up when, in a remote outpost, a mentally deranged bombardier killed our excellent battery commander, Captain Evans, with a burst from a Sterling sub machine gun, six feet from where I was standing. Being unarmed at the time, I had to take swift evasive action to avoid suffering the same fate. What happened next is for another memoir.

A few weeks before 1st Field Battery was due to rejoin the rest of 14th Field Regiment in Hong Kong, I read on the orderly room notice board at Seedaseer Lines that the Trucial Oman Scouts were looking for a volunteer Army Catering Corps NCO. The TOS were spoken about with some awe amongst us common soldiery in Aden, so, heavily over-dosed on boys' own adventure stories, I put my name down. Most of my friends thought I was 'macnoon'- 'mad'.
  'You're off your trolley. Aden's the backside of the world- and you want to go about a thousand miles up it?'
  'You've been out in the sun too long, mate.' Etcetera.

About five months passed before I was sent for by a clerk in the Battery Office at Sek Kong Camp in the New Territories and told I had been accepted by the TOS. If I hadn't changed my mind, I had four days in which to get ready to leave. My travel orders would take me by sea to Aden; on to Bahrain by 'plane, then to Sharjah. I was to wear civilian clothing throughout the journey. Suits me!
  Travelling alone, I had no-one to give me orders on the Oxfordshire. Ignored by all in authority, I was free to enjoy a very pleasant two weeks cruise across the Indian Ocean. Someone knew of my existence, though, because when the troopship anchored in Aden's harbour on Christmas Eve, an RAF launch promptly came along side to collect and deliver me to a Land Rover waiting on a jetty at Steamer Point. The deserted transit camp was nothing more than a cluster of dusty marquees, close enough to Khormaksar Airport to be made even dustier whenever a 'plane took off.
  Spending Christmas alone was not a very cheerful prospect. I felt the only thing for me to do was to go to one of my old haunts, the Rock Hotel in Steamer Point, get seriously drunk and blot everything out for a couple of days.

I could have taken one of the taxis waiting for customers outside the gates of Seedaseer and Singapore Lines, but with time hanging heavy on my hands, I decided to walk. It was damned hot trudging along the shoreline, heading for the point where I would be obliged to leave it and take the road through Maalla.
  The sight of all that surf tumbling onto the sand eventually became too much for me. I needed to cool off in that water! Intense loneliness can addle the brain; without a second thought, I removed shoes, socks, shirt and slacks, stuffing my wrist watch into a pocket containing, what was for me, a large amount of East African shillings.

It was a short swim, but an expensive one. When I returned to my clothing I soon discovered that my watch and money had been stolen – in fact, everything had gone from my pockets - even my comb! Some opportunist had taken advantage of my stupidity, although there wasn't a soul in sight to indicate who it may have been. With no hope of being able to get an advance on my pay, or gain access to my savings until well after Christmas, I returned gloomily to the transit camp and consoled myself by writing to a girl I'd never met, but had been exchanging letters with for about a year. Her name was Daphne. I had seen her stunning photograph in a British newspaper. It accompanied an article about youth clubs. An out-of-date copy came up with the mail to where 1st Field Battery had been camped in the Radfan Mountains. Not knowing the girl's address, I had sent an open letter to the newspaper and asked them to forward it to her. She replied after a while; her mother having nagged her to, 'Write to that poor boy out in the desert.'

Good fortune smiled on me. A small group of Argyll and Sutherland Highlanders turned up at the transit camp. Like me, they were waiting for a flight to Bahrain. They very kindly bought me a few beers at the NAAFI Club, and when we finally arrived in Bahrain, insisted that I spend Hogmanay with them at their barracks, rather than stay the night at the Speedbird Hotel. Being the guest of a Scottish regiment at Hogmanay turned out to be an unforgettable experience!

Swooping and soaring on thermals, a Twin Pioneer aircraft took me the three hundred, or so, miles to Sharjah. Judging from what I saw while coming in to land, it had also taken me back a couple of hundred years. After coming in low over Sharjah, an ancient, straggling town that had lost whatever importance it may have had, when its creek silted up, we bounced to a halt on hard-packed sand beside a fort with a 1930's style control tower at one end. Rudyard Kipling and Lord Roberts would have both felt quite at home in the Trucial Oman Scouts camp. It appeared to have been left over from the days of the Raj. A pair of ancient cannon stood in front of the verandah-ed HQ building. The parade ground (more hard-packed sand) was delineated by white painted stones and the billets were straight out of 'Gunga Din'
.

Replete with stingrays and sinister snakes
A poisonous sea lapped up against
A salt encrusted stagnant shore.
Suspended fish hung drying there.
Tainting the overheated air –
Malodorous vapours under a ruthless glare.
Adobe-walled dwellings, mosaic-tiled floors,
Cooling towers and compounds
With scorpion-locked doors.**
A straggling town with a barusti-roofed souk;
Gold, silver, myrrh and a lantern wick.
Camelus Dromedarius and a camel-stick,

**Cast iron locks, shaped like scorpions. Removing the tail locked the door.

With fellow Bollywood film fan, Cpl Gordon Nunns RAPC (on the right)

I had already made a couple of irrational decisions in my young life. Leaving home to live and work in hotels at the age of fifteen, I had been determined to join the army at the earliest opportunity; even turning down a job on Lord and Lady Docker's yacht, Shemara, to do so when I was seventeen and a half. Now I had left the sybaritic pleasures of Hong Kong to be in this desolate, furnace-hot place. I could almost hear my father's voice saying, 'You never learn, do you!?'

I was told to report to the commander of the TOS, Colonel Stewart Carter. Looking for all the world like the famous, 'stiff upper lip', Hollywood actor, C Aubrey Smith, the colonel's powerful personality filled his office like a live thing as he welcomed me to the force and informed me that I was 'on my own'. The commander's responsibilities lay with his Arab soldiers He expected, indeed, demanded that British volunteers carry out their duties efficiently and take care of themselves. If they failed to do so, they would not last long in the TOS.

The occupants of Billet 306 lifted my spirits. With only one or two exceptions, here was a group of remarkably civilised junior NCOs. This may sound pompous, but it is true to say they were a cut above most of those I had encountered in the army so far. I soon discovered that this could be said about virtually all of the British volunteers which included a handful of Royal Army Pay Corps National Servicemen. They were an indication that regulars serving in the pay corps were reluctant to join us!

Others will agree that the force attracted the eccentric, the ever so slightly mad, the wild and the downright reckless, but most of them possessed the capacity, some may say, the strength of character, to remain good humoured while carrying out their duties under extremely difficult conditions, or when the drink flowed, which it sometimes did. Drunken punch-ups were not for them; abrasive wit and risky stunts being more their style when they were 'in their cups'.

With the sand crumbling from beneath our wheels we bailed out at this point.

As for myself, I sometimes felt that my service in the TOS was something akin to being an extra in one of those sprawling, Alexander Korda movies set in the old British Empire. Gordon Nunns went to the trouble and expense of importing what, at the time, may well have been the only bicycle in the Trucial States. In those days there wasn't an inch of tarmac road in the whole territory - or for that matter, any other kind of road. Mostly, one made one's own track when travelling to the outstations or going on exercise. Gordon was quite content with riding his bike around the camp; he had to be, there was nothing but rutted sand beyond it. We both had an interest in films; and as a consequence, although it wasn't recommended to do so, we would sometimes make our way at night to what passed for an open-air cinema in Sharjah. Simple in the extreme, it consisted of rows of wooden benches and a frame-work upon which a temporary screen could be suspended. Some sort of generator, brought in on the back of the battered truck powered the projector. Trying to look as 'Arab' as possible, Gordon and I would buy our one rupee tickets and watch endless Indian movies, scarcely understanding a word that was being spoken but enjoying the visual drama, comedy and inevitable song and dance routines. On more than one occasion we were spotted as being 'Kafirs' and forced to beat a hasty retreat as an offended local waved his camel stick about and began to rouse the rest of the audience against us.

Apart from Hong Kong, and before that, a brief spell at Barford Camp, near Barnard Castle, I'd had little opportunity to practice whatever skills I possessed as an Officers' Mess chef, and I never had the chance to do so with the TOS. The officers maintained their tradition of employing Arab cooks, so I was promoted to the rank of corporal and given the job of running the sergeants' mess kitchen, which was little more than an ill-equipped shack with barusti walls (made from the wood and leaves of the date palm) through which the sand blew freely, and a galvanized metal roof which I could easily have fried eggs on in the heat of day! I had learned to be inventive with composite rations while serving in Aden; this, together with an intermittent supply of fresh food, kept the ebullient bunch of senior NCOs reasonably happy. My two assistants in the kitchen were a Goanese man and an Arab boy. We got on well together. The Goanese, whose name I'm ashamed to say I have forgotten, invited me back to his home in Sharjah, from time to time. He had a charming wife and two delightful children. They lived in dire poverty so I was always moved by their kind hospitality. He was eventually to suffer a severe flogging while strapped to the cannon that stood outside the Sheikh of Sharjah's palace, for stealing some trinkets in order to raise enough money to buy penicillin for his sick daughter. I'm sure our medics would have helped him out if he'd asked them.

   One of the sergeants had a goat which he kept in a purpose-built compound. It was missing when he returned from a trip up country. Some of his friends had thought it would be a great joke if they turned the animal into a curry. After they'd taunted him about this, the sergeant gained his revenge by driving a panic stricken donkey into the crowded mess.
   'Curry that, you bastards,' he yelled, as it careered about, knocking over tables and chairs and creating general chaos. I took every opportunity to travel about the Trucial States, preferring to be out on an exercise or even acting as a volunteer pay roll guard on trips to the out stations, when I was free to do so.   Then there were the rest and recreation trips to the virtually deserted island of Abu Musa, which lay in the approaches to the Straits of Hormuz.

   Bombardier Hopkins was adamant! Only a fool suffers discomfort when he can avoid it, so there was no way he was going to Abu Musa for a long weekend without taking his bed with him. Sleeping on the ground, wrapped in a couple of blankets, or lying on a charpoy, the bottom of which was apt to rest on stony ground, was not for him. He wanted to take the bed out of his billet and that was that! It was duly loaded onto a Bedford, along with supplies sufficient for the five of us. We bounced our merry way to the quay, opposite the officer's mess in Sharjah, where the dhow, Al Qaid, awaited with its Arab crew.
   With everything stowed, and the bed standing proudly on deck, we were soon enjoying the pleasures of a dhow trip. The sea was calm, the sun shone and fish gave themselves up to our hand lines. Using a fire built within a cut-away oil drum, I quickly converted some of them into an almost edible curry. As we ate, we watched a school of sleek porpoises flashing ahead of the Al Qaid, slicing their way through the phosphorescent sea.

   The change in the weather came remarkably quickly. One minute all was plain sailing, so to speak, the next, we were plunging through a considerable swell. There was no rain, but the wind increased its strength as we approached Abu Musa, making it too dangerous to attempt to go anywhere near the stone jetty that had been constructed by Germans before the First World War when they were mining red ochre. We dropped anchor, hoped it would hold, and waited.
   The stormy conditions continued unabated, so we were obliged to spend the night aboard the dhow. As darkness fell, a plague of wildlife emerged from its woodwork. The boat was soon swarming with beetles, cockroaches and other insect life as we lay on its pitching deck, trying to get some shuteye. The guy who'd brought his bed with him was literally above all this - he was rocked to sleep, undisturbed, on his own, firmly anchored, bed!
   Putting to one side that tempting cliché, 'It was a dark and stormy night' I resort to, 'Came the dawn'.

With a huge swell still running, our sensible and experienced Arab crew still refused to approach the jetty. We wanted to get on to that island!

Our eyes fell upon the tiny rowboat that had trailed in our wake, at the end of a rope, all the way from Sharjah. Rising and falling on a heaving sea we brought the small boat alongside. The bed was lowered on ropes until it straddled the small craft. Two or three of us swarmed down to it.

Well overloaded, we were swept towards a tiny wedge of beach at the foot of a crumbling cliff and dumped like flotsam on the sand by a contemptuous wave.

We unloaded the wretched bed and two brave souls made the difficult return to the dhow in order to bring back our supplies and the remainder of the party, who made a similarly exciting trip to shore. Our last task involved hauling the bed to the top of the cliff. It was a triumphal moment for us when it stood in all its glory on the island of Abu Musa.

Shades of R M Ballantyne's, 'Coral Island'! Apart from the remains of a short length of narrow gauge railway track and some abandoned wagons, once used to bring red ochre from the quarry to the jetty, there was no hint of civilisation here. This island belonged to the lizards and seabirds. We borrowed it for a few days of swimming, fishing and climbing to its highest point, Mount Halva, which, at only four hundred feet high, hardly deserves its title.

RSM Henderson was given a Christmas present. After a little bit of bribery, the RAF guards were persuaded to allow a small aircraft, I forget what type, to be pulled from the airfield in the middle of the night and parked, festooned with Christmas greetings, as close to his billet door as possible, for him to discover when he woke up on Christmas morning.

After learning that a small unit of British paratroopers was out in the desert, five or six of us got together and decided to raid their camp. Their exact position having been obtained by some means or other, we 'acquired' a vehicle and set off to find them. All we had to do was infiltrate their camp at night, write the letters TOS all over their vehicles, using sticks of chalk, and get out again.Our simple strategy was to split up, get as close as possible to where the paratroopers were laagered, wait for darkness- and go in.

I crawled along a shallow wadi to within about fifty yards of the target. They had circled their vehicles and two guards had been posted. Thoughts of wagon trains waiting for the Indians to attack crossed my juvenile mind. Night fell, but the moon was too bright for my liking. I didn't stand a chance of crossing the fifty yards to their perimeter without being seen. The guards were circling the camp in opposite directions, stopping to exchange a few words as they passed each other. I made a decision when their paths crossed and they stood talking together. I stood up, urinated, then, with most of my face wrapped in camo, I strolled straight into the camp as though I belonged there. The guards ignored me; but not when I crouched down in the darkness, hidden away, beside a Land Rover and attempted to write TOS on one of its doors. I didn't think to lick the stick of chalk; consequently, it made a hideous screeching sound as I attempted the downward stroke of the letter T on the metal work, bringing the guards rushing over. I stood up rather hastily when I heard them cock their Sterlings.

'Good evening,' I said, in the best plummy accent I could muster.

Two cheerful, armed to the teeth, hitch-hikers we found yomping across the desert while we were on our way to our unofficial night raid on the Para camp.

Although the paras muttered dire threats about what they would like to do to me, they left me alone. Paddy Farelly and John Ashworth were also captured. Ashworth had a rifle butt rammed painfully into his guts. He wasn't happy about it. The officer in charge provided us with mugs of tea and kept us bottled up in a tent until the moon was down then threw us out.

We had to cross a low range of hills to get to where we had left the one tonner. With no moon to light our way, it was a difficult hike. A lot of swearing and cursing could be heard as one or the other of us stumbled over rocks, fell into gullies or encountered thorn bushes.

When we re-joined the remaining members of our little expedition, we found that while the paras had been busy with us, they had been busy too; writing TOS on everything they could find, before strolling back to the lorry in the moonlight and enjoying a 'brew-up'. They had been thoughtful enough to flash the vehicle's headlights from time to time, in the hope that we were out there somewhere and it would help guide us in. It did.

Towards the end of my tour, it looked to me as though the TOS was in danger of becoming as 'regimental' as any traditional British army unit. Unappealing concrete barrack blocks had been built outside the old camp. To a certain degree, their single rooms broke up the, 'we're all in it together', camaraderie that existed in the original rough and ready camp. A new style commander had arrived, together with a punctilious RSM. One thing was certain, there would be no chance of him taking over from me to finish digging a rubbish pit out in the desert, as RSM Henderson had done on a fiercely hot day, after I'd ignored his advice to put my shemagh on, and had been overcome by the heat. I was only 'out' for a minute or two, but when I came to my senses in the shade of a tent; there he was, digging away – and there were no recriminations afterwards!

A Medal Award Parade in 1961; Political Agent, James Craig, shakes hands with the Sheikh of Sharjah. COMTOS, Col. Bartholomew, is on horseback

Coming in for a ration drop during an operation

   Love conquers all, they say. It certainly conquered me when I first met Daphne on my mid-tour leave! She arranged to meet me off a train at her local station. I had this romantic vision of myself, the bronzed young hero returning home from foreign parts, emerging from a cloud of steam and engine smoke and into the arms of a beautiful girl waiting for me on the platform. It wasn't quite like that.

For one thing, it was an electrified railway line, so away went the steam and smoke - and for another- the platform was deserted when I alighted. Daphne was late because she'd been unable to decide what dress to wear! The only thing I'd got right in my vision was that Daphne was breathtakingly beautiful

> 'We walked beside burgeoning hedgerows
> Under an English August sun,
> She with tolerant amusement
> Allowing my braggart tongue to run on;
> But it was my heart that raced far ahead of us
> As we arrived at her garden gate;
> For I knew with an utter certitude
> That here was my love, my life, my fate.'

Four more years were to pass before we married.

Back with the TOS, my twenty first birthday was well celebrated! Someone had a guitar. A rough and ready double bass was constructed out of a large box, a length of wood and some stiff wire. The timpani section was provided by an oil drum and various bottles and cans. With beer being the creative force, we made a lovely noise!

I remember – I remember: a desert landscape transformed into a brief floral delight after rare rainfall; swarms of locusts darkening the sky: the unfailing hospitality of the Arabs one encountered along the way. A small group of tribesmen in some far-off place I was visiting, unselfconsciously entertaining themselves by performing a traditional knife dance to music being played on a wind-up gramophone; a camel caravan, silhouetted on the horizon: me, wandering away from a night camp until it was out of sight, to stand beneath an enormous canopy of stars and listen to the silence, while imagining in that fanciful way I had, that I might be the first European to visit the spot. But most of all, I remember the comradeship.

I may have made service in the TOS sound too pleasurable. This is because I have no wish to dwell on the sometimes unbearable climate, the occasional dramas, the bed bugs, salt water showers, lack of fresh water in general, and battling against the eternal desert on practically every journey one made. I could also mention, among other things, the grim, archaic working conditions for any self-respecting chef, the ever encroaching sand, the monotonous diet and the total lack of female companionship; although one senior NCO temporarily solved this last problem for himself by smuggling an air hostess from Bahrain into a desert outpost!
Then there were the flies;
> 'Oh little fly upon the wall,
> Ain't you got no folks at all?
> Ain't you got no mum and dad?
> SMACK goes the hand----   Then die, you bastard!'

The Foreign Office was, I believe, thinking ahead. They knew the old days were fading fast. Oil was just beginning to flow in large quantities. The Trucial States would become rich. A larger and more fully equipped force would soon be necessary to help police the region. That air of informality and self regulation I loved so much began to slowly dissipate. So, with a mixture of sorrow and relief, I decided not to sign on for a second tour.

I was offered a choice of two postings. I could either be a shift NCO in the kitchens at Shepton Mallet Military Prison, or become personal chef to the GOC, Wales District; living and working in a fine house, with lawns sweeping down to the River Wye, four miles from Builth Wells.

In a very bizarre contrast to the life I'd been living, I was soon dealing with freshly caught salmon and shot - riddled pheasants, brought in to the kitchen and slapped on to the table by a dour, Welsh gamekeeper, or waiting for the general's wife to press a button in the dining room. It activated a bell in the kitchen to notify me that it was time to put the cheese soufflés in the oven! It was a far cry from cooking chapattis on hot stones and drinking brackish water from a goat-skin bag.

Oh, and Daphne and I are still living happily ever after.

Next; as an addendum to this chapter: Roger Davies RAPC, one of the five National Servicemen who volunteered to serve with the TOS, records his experiences.

The TOS football team 1961. Colonel Carter at front row, centre

NATIONAL SERVICEMEN FILL THE BREACH

Roger Davies RAPC

I feel privileged to have been one of only five National Servicemen to have served in the Trucial Oman Scouts. Corporal Norman, Private Cameron and myself were asked if we would like to do so. In March 1961, we were joined by Privates Len Ormond and Archie McNaught

At this time the Trucial Oman Scouts HQ was still in its original camp just outside Sharjah. The Training Centre and Depot for Arab recruits was at Manama. The Desert Regiment and Mortar Troop were based at Idhin. Other Squadrons were based at Fort Jahili, Masafi, Mirfa and Al Khatt.

On the 26th Feb 1961, we had a visit from Archbishop Campbell from Jerusalem and afterwards were allowed to accompany him and his entourage to partake of refreshments at the Political Residency in Dubai.

Many of us based at the Sharjah garrison found that sport was an excellent form of relaxation. The TOS had several different sports teams, including football, cricket - and darts! Thanks to the generosity of the Nuffield Foundation, who donated the equipment, we were also able to try our hand at archery. The football team played in the Trucial States league, which was organised by Flight Lieutenant J Cobbold RAF. The RAF had two teams, The Wanderers and The Canaries. The other teams were the TOS, the cavalry squadrons who rotated on three months detachment from Aden, Dubai Union A and B teams, Sharjah Town, Young Sharjah and B.P. The TOS team was composed of a mixed bag of British and Arab personnel. The Wanderers were the dominant team in my time.

When Bob Cameron and myself were on the brink of finishing our tour of duty with the TOS, the Arab soldiers who played in the TOS team, requested a game against the British. We managed to win by the narrow margin of 3-2.

The TOS pay office provided four members for the football and cricket teams, Bruce Norman, who was an exceptional footballer and cricketer, Bob Cameron, Len Ormond and myself. The commander of the TOS, Colonel Bartholomew was a very keen cricketer and a good batsman. He was a regular member of the TOS team. Both our football and cricket teams went on a tour of Bahrain with limited success. Captain Fraser arranged a rugby match in Kuwait which I, and many others, were looking forward to. It was cancelled at the last minute when Iraq threatened to invade the country. Sharjah became a sudden hive of activity, with a squadron of Canberra Bombers and Javelin Fighters on the airfield and the TOS billets cramped with Inniskillings when they arrived from Nairobi and were billeted with us. The emergency was short lived; the Royal Navy, RAF and Army units being quickly deployed elsewhere.

After the AOR's versus BOR's football match on June 7th 1961
The BOR's won by 3 goals to 2

At the end of 1961, members of the TOS were sent to assist with locust control. The locusts, a sight to behold as they blackened the sky and made the ground appear to be moving, caused extensive damage in Ras Al Khaimah and Buraimi.

On Jan 10th 1962, the Secretary of State for War, John Profumo, inspected the TOS HQ at Sharjah. He was accompanied by his wife, Valerie Hobson, the former film star, and Brigadier Bryars, OC Land Forces, Persian Gulf. This was shortly before the 'Profumo Affair' scandal involving a Russian agent, Christine Keeler, Mandy Rice-Davies and Stephen Ward, erupted. Our Paymaster, Major Tibbey, delegated me to follow the official party, along with a bevy of army reporters and photographers, because of my job I knew the names of those being interviewed.

10th January 1962.
A guard of honour for Secretary of State for War, John Profumo, at Fort Jahili

John Profumo and his wife, the actress, Valerie Hobson, inspecting a falaj at Buraimi

7

BANISHED FROM SHARJAH!

Robert Lines Grenadier Guards

AS IT WAS IN THE BEGINNING.

  Having served in the Grenadier Guards in 'Public Duties and Instructing' at the Training Battalion camp at Pirbright, I was growing despondent at not obtaining an overseas posting. Having discussed the problem with the powers that be, I was left in no doubt that I was not going anywhere. Then I discovered a Trucial Oman Scouts recruiting poster. I surreptitiously volunteered to join them. Months later, to the annoyance of the aforesaid regimental powers, I was told I'd been accepted.

  My travel orders took me to Southampton and the Troopship Devonshire, which was bound for the Far East via Aden. Two Scottish infantry battalions were also on board, bound for Hong Kong. Teaming up with some RAF chaps, who, like me, were going to Aden, I avoided any form of duty, including joining the infantry in tiresome drills and physical exercises; concentrating instead on sunbathing on the upper deck, watching the sea slide by as we headed for Gibraltar, the Suez Canal and the Red Sea. As a matter of interest, as punishment for the havoc they'd caused in Gibraltar, the Scottish battalions were refused shore leave when we reached Aden.

Deposited on the quay with those RAF bods, I watched them depart in a truck while wondering what I was supposed to do next. After a while, two military policemen turned up and demanded to know why I was hanging about. It soon became apparent that no-one in Aden knew, or cared about my presence.

The Arab Language School where I was supposed to have been booked into for a crash course, had never heard of me, but they allowed me on the course.

After a month of study, it was decided that I was ready for Sharjah and the TOS. One morning, just before dawn, I boarded the RAF single engine, mail delivery plane at Khormaksar. It was a rather daunting, but exhilarating flight, following the coast line and stopping at outposts that Her Majesty probably didn't even know she possessed! Al Mukalla, Salalah and Masirah.
In Muscat, having spent several hours without food, I made the mistake of eating several bananas. I felt distinctly queasy as we continued flying above the desert on the last leg of the trip. Astonishingly, I had managed to travel all the way from the UK without a passport!

Colonel Hugh Bartholomew COMTOS

The day after my arrival I was marched in to the presence of the commanding officer, Colonel Bartholomew, to be interviewed. Sideburns, shemagh and sun tan welcomed me enthusiastically. I was, apparently, his long awaited new Sais. I indicated that I had no idea what that was.
A GROOM FOR THE STABLES!?

As I explained to the colonel when he asked me how much I knew about horses, I didn't know one end of the animals from the other! His face turned red-scarlet- crimson, I thought he was going to explode. He bellowed at me,
'What the hell can you do, then?'
I told him that, as a Grenadier guard, I was very good at drill. I could 'left turn', 'right turn' and come to a halt with the best of 'em. The colonel finished shouting at me and began shouting at the RSM instead.
'Get him out of here! Send him up to Manama and don't let him come back!'
Yet another cock-up! On my TOS application form, no-one had noticed that the requirement was for a Horse Guard, not a foot slogging Grenadier! I was fortunate not to be returned to my unit.

BANISHED TO MANAMA!

Within hours, I was driving through the desert towards Manama Training Depot. I arrived there in the dark, was shown to my barusti hut, flopped onto my bed and fell asleep.
I was woken up the next morning by what sounded like a ships' foghorn. It turned out to be a braying donkey standing forlornly at the foot of the nearby jebel. Welcome to Manama!
Upon examining my accommodation in daylight, I could see that my barusti hut consisted of four wooden poles, with walls made from intertwined palm leaves, connecting them. There was a doorway - but no door. It was to be my home for several months.

My barusti hut at Manama

Having trained British soldiers for long periods, it was an eye-opener to find myself standing in front of one hundred Arab recruits. Some were locals, but others came from areas as far distant as the Hadhramaut and Dhofar; a motley group of youngsters. When the Quartermaster arrived from Sharjah with a lorry load of army uniforms to issue to the recruits, it was fascinating to watch them wrestling with European clothing for the first time in their young lives.
Our Arab instructors all had previous experience. I had been allocated to Sergeant Ali bin Sultan. I have no hesitation in saying he was a very good instructor - and friend. Without him, I would not have been able to produce some of the excellent squads of men we did. Corporal Obaid Ali was another up-and-coming young soldier.

Sergeant Robert Lines at Manama

Accommodation at Manama could not have been more basic. We erected marquee tents, lined up in military fashion. The recruits were issued with charpoy beds, but seldom used them for their proper purpose. They found it was easier to sleep on the desert floor and leave their kit laid out on the bed, ready for the morning inspection! The camp was situated at the base of the range of hills that swept down from North Oman to the volcanic plain that continued into the desert country. The site had been chosen because there was clean water there. It seldom rained, but when it did, it was torrential, pouring out of the hills and filling every wadi. It once rained so hard the whole camp, including tents and offices built from barusti, were swept away. Only a few pre-fabricated buildings were left standing. It had played havoc, flattening the whole place. We spent several days cleaning up the camp. As some compensation, the sun helped dry everything out rather quickly and the whole area became temporarily transformed from arid desert to green oasis. No dust for days and the local wadis were suddenly full of bird life, with pools of water collected in the rocky areas. On the down-side, the desert tracks were impassable.

Next, it was creating a firing range. After choosing an area away from any desert track, we used sand dunes as butts and measured out one hundred metres from them to mark a firing point. Trunks of palm trees formed a base line, with rocks strategically placed on top of them to accommodate up to ten firing points. Sand bags in the front of this crude structure made it workable. We dug holes at the butts and reverted more sand bags into them to support our home made wooden 4x4 targets. Hey, presto! We had a two hundred metre firing range! Months later, a couple of bulldozers were sent up from Sharjah to make us proper firing points and butts. A major brought his Squadron up to Manama to have their weapons 'zeroed'. At dawn the next morning, the first testing shots were fired. After spending hours zeroing in weapons, I was invited to the major's tent. He offered me some refreshments. Being very thirsty, I took a long drink from a bottle the major handed me, only stopping when I realised I was gulping down pure gin. I declined to eat his curry, bade him farewell, and with eyes watering and belly bubbling, left him to his repast.

Passing out parade. Another excellent squad of soldiers

Talking of food, whenever possible, I took the opportunity to do some sight-seeing and fishing; the sea being only a few hours drive across country. In those days, the coast was a paradise of deserted, beautiful beaches with plenty of wild life: turtles, sharks, flamingoes - and pigeons, (which made a decent meal if you could shoot enough of them).

Laying out kit for new recruits

Tactical training always took place in areas far from the Depot; near water and, whenever possible, close to some delightful tented Arab hospitality. By this time I was able to speak 'Jaish' (Military) Arabic quite well.

Marquees lined up with military precision

A young Arab Lieutenant, Sheikh Faisal bin Sultan al Qasimi, joined the depot on attachment, prior to going to the UK on a language course. We had met previously at his wedding, which took place at a village called, Al Khatt, quite close to Manama.

A high-born Arab's wedding is fantastic to say the least. I arrived in the middle of the afternoon. A huge number of tents had been erected across the dunes and hundreds of guests were milling about; singing, dancing and enjoying camel races.

After sunset, the only light came from myriads of camp fires. Sweet aromas filled the air. It was like an enchanting scene from 'A Thousand and One Nights'. Unfortunately, we few Brits, who'd had the privilege of being invited to this wondrous, never to be forgotten, affair, had to return to camp rather earlier than we wanted to. We had work to do! Later, we were told that the wedding lasted for four days.

Wedding celebrations would go on for four days

We built a runway in the desert. It was back-breaking work, cutting down prolific thorn trees and bushes before loading them onto lorries for disposal.

Considering the climate, clearing an area several hundred metres long and a hundred wide was no mean feat. We worked with the most basic of tools; hatchets, machetes and a few spades. After that was accomplished, the whole area had to be graded and the perimeter marked by large stones which we covered in white paint to help guide the pilots.

After doing a roll call one day, before heading back to camp, one of the new recruits was missing. Had he deserted? Got lost? No. I found him, still working at the top of the runway. He had been asked to check for holes around the perimeter and had become so engrossed, he was singing to himself while he lifted each and every stone, one at a time, along the whole line. Ah well?

We gave some newly-arrived British personnel an introductory trip around the Sheikhdoms. There were still no roads, only well worn desert tracks. One made one's way, from Dubai to Abu Dhabi, along the sea shore. Abu Dhabi was surrounded by sea and little more than a fishing village. The TOS camp at Tariff was right on the beach!

` A squad of new recruits, attached to Musafi's 'X' Squadron, were deployed to a problem area. There had been a confrontation between two tribes, the Shuhu and the more local Dibba people. They were both 'claiming' rights to a particular well. It was an age-old problem that frequently ended up with people being killed – leading to further feuding.

The Mafia had nothing on them! On this occasion, with 'X' Squadron away, dealing with trouble elsewhere, the recruits intervened, taking control of the wells. Their presence ensured that the situation ended peacefully - until the next time.

We built a runway in the desert

. Pioneering oil men in the area entertained us with fine food and drink; a cut above what we'd grown used to. Then it was on to Burami Oasis, where camel trains stopped to water and feed before moving on to different Sheikdoms. Fort Jahili, standing proud in the desert, and Jebal Hafit were wonderful sights to be seen before the long drive back to Manama, via the Fia gap.

One last memory; we held a Christmas Eve Draw at the Sharjah Sergeants' Mess. After all the prizes had been won, we resorted to cutting the RAF Station's senior warrant officer's bicycle into pieces and presenting it to him as the last prize.

On the firing range

. ;

At dawn the next morning, a race ensued to beat the Commanding Officer of the TOS to Manama. He was flying there to wish everyone at the camp a happy Christmas. We were using a three-ton Bedford, and all hung over and thirsty. We were in such a state, in fact, that we forgot we had piled several crates of beer in the back of the lorry before the hi-jinks started the previous evening.

Despite risking life and limb in that lorry, the Qaid (commander TOS) flew over us just before we reached Manama. We found him drinking beer in the small room that passed as a mess. We succumbed again to hard drinking and a Christmas party of note.

We went to Dubai from time to time, via a track that crossed a stretch of desert that frequently displayed shimmering mirages. These trips were made to use our ration allowances to buy food and other essentials as we had to cater for ourselves. We had to keep the two excellent Pakistani cooks we had at Manama, supplied with basic items.

It was possible to buy long-playing records at Jashanmals, the only modern store in Dubai. We had a record player in the mess, but we usually ended up hurling the discs at each other in frisby-style duels. Inevitably on these trips, we would end up visiting the Sharjah Sergeants' Mess; getting rowdy before driving made for a rather hazardous, not to say bilious drive back to Manama

Tactical training

Celebrating Eids (Arab holidays) were good for the morale of recruits and instructors alike. Rifles were issued, along with a few rounds of ammunition, so that the soldiers could temporarily revert to their traditional method of celebrating; marching round with much Bedouin singing and dancing, twirling their rifles round their heads and firing them into the air.

Rapid fire-commence!

Sheikh Faisal bin Sultan al Qasimi with Col F. de Butts

They were happy days! I felt a real sense of pride and happiness over my achievement as an instructor as my tour of duty came to an end. A new company commander, Major Kerwin, arrived, along with Sergeant Gordon Bell and Sergeant Paddy Boulin. It didn't take me long to discover that I was leaving the recruits in very good hands.

Editor's note:
       In 1965, the British government of the day announced its intentions to withdraw from the Persian Gulf. Although it was to continue for a further six years, this spelt the end for the Trucial Oman Scouts. Some time before that happened, the Emir of Abu Dhabi, suddenly wealthy through oil, promptly formed the Abu Dhabi Defence Force in order to protect his own interests. Here, with his kind permission, is an edited extract from 'Life', the autobiography of Dennis Shiels, one of the Trucial Oman Scouts NCOs who helped train the Abu Dhabi Defence Force.

ADDF Section within the UAE Military Museum display in the Armed Forces Officers' Club IN Abu Dhabi

8

TRAINING THE ABU DHABI DEFENCE FORCE

Dennis Shiels Royal Lancashire Fusiliers

In 1964, some weeks before our battalion of Lancashire Fusiliers were due to return home from Georgetown, British Guyana, I was sent for by the Adjutant who told me that a posting to the Trucial Oman Scouts that I had applied for had come through. Did I still want it?

I soon found myself on Atkinson Field with a large send-off party on their way to hangovers. After leave in the UK, I flew to Aden where I studied Arabic at the School of Middle East Languages. Only one other member of my class was bound for Sharjah and the Trucial Oman Scouts; the rest of them were joining the Federal Regular Army in Aden. We were temporarily accommodated in the Sergeants' Mess at Waterloo Lines, where we took on some night duties. The New Year's Eve Party had been cancelled for some reason, so, on a night during which I happened to be on duty, they held a Dinner-Dance. During the course of the evening, a young corporal came to see me. Something suspicious had been spotted in an air-conditioning unit I went along to investigate and saw a greenish substance jammed in the intake.

I couldn't see it very well – and I certainly had no intention of touching it! I cleared everyone out of the barrack block, including the Sergeants' Mess; stopping the dancers in mid fox trot.

Then I telephoned the bomb disposal unit. I also alerted the Army Fire Service, the Military Police and the Medical Team. They all attended the scene.

After members of the Bomb Disposal Unit had cautiously poked around for an hour or so, to my embarrassment, they concluded that the substance was actually the remains of a tin of composite ration cheese! Everybody left after casting doubts on my parentage. The days were numbered for the Trucial Oman Scouts by the time I got to them. My role was, in fact, to help train the brand new, Abu Dhabi Defence Force.

The Sheikh of Abu Dhabi's son was sent to the UK with a large amount of money to buy stores and equipment. He had a very good time, but returned with masses of useless items that simply went to waste; apart, that is, from a bolt of the best barathea cloth that money could buy. I engaged a local tailor to make three uniforms from it for the Sheikh, each one had three stars on the shoulder straps to indicate that the wearer was a captain squadron commander.

His father; a real Bedouin Sheikh, paid us a visit. He appeared, dressed in traditional garb, topped with a European jacket and wearing a rather battered pair of brown shoes, laced up with string. He was newly-rich, but, being unused to great wealth, asked the price of every little thing! Our commandant being away, it was left to me to try and answer his questions about the financial aspects of the new defence force. He accepted my answers, but was adamant that his son was not going to remain a mere captain, answerable to foreigners. He brought about his resignation and made him Abu Dhabi's defence minister!

It was essential that the ADDF receive desert training. It wasn't easy to provide them with it, though. Thanks to the parsimonious sheikh, we only had three vehicles and only one of those was in a serviceable condition. On our first desert exercise, most of us were obliged to make a long and exhausting trek back to our barracks on foot. After a while, we were able to obtain some decent vehicles from the Trucial Oman Scouts.

An interesting event, though not a particularly pleasant one, occurred one morning when I set out to inspect the Squadron before work commenced. I found that a large number of men were absent from parade. At the time, we were sleeping in the open air, that is, without tents. After searching for the absentees, I found them and quickly realized they were unfit for work. They all had high temperatures. There were some shallow ditches, called falajes, nearby, used to channel water from a nearby oasis. It ran cool, clean and clear, so I was able to make use of that to help reduce their temperatures. Then I commandeered everyone's spare shirts and tacked them together to make them a rough and ready shelter from the sun.

After detailing a few troops to look after their sick friends, I went off in search of a mission hospital I'd been told about. I found it eventually. The people there were very kind to me, but being run on a charity shoestring, they had little medication to spare for a casual caller. The principals were the Doctors Kennedy, a married couple. They provided me with as much aspirin as they could spare and some useful advice. They suspected that the sick men had measles, which could cause them to have pulmonary problems. Regular doses of aspirin and plenty of liquid were the order of the day.

1966- The Abu Dhabi Defence Force - all four of them!!

On my way back to camp, I called in at a barusti shack in Buraimi, where I thought I might be able to buy some sort of cordial to make the water more palatable for my patients. I was startled to find that the rear wall of the place had case after case of Vimto stacked against it! When I explained to the ancient Arab who ran the show that Vimto was made near where I lived in England and I needed a quantity of it for my sick soldiers, he let me have what I wanted for a bargain price. In those days, a simple thing like a few bottles of juice could make all the difference. That Vimto certainly improved my patients' morale. Quite often, one of our group had to go down to Sharjah or Dubai to pick up stores and rations. It meant setting out at about four o' clock in the morning.

Being sat next to a monosyllabic Arab driver before dawn may not appear to be much fun, but I always found it to be to my liking. I enjoyed the feeling of insularity -- sat in the darkened cab while the world we were passing through was revealed in our headlights. I loved the dark velvet lure of the hard-packed sand road and the changing colours brought about by the dawn; blue-black to soft, salmon pink then on to a bright golden yellow. The complete spectrum of spectacular colours was ours to enjoy throughout the day.

The ground on both sides of the track was sometimes a mass of colour as well. Low growing, begonia-type flowers creating purple and yellow carpets as far as the eye could see. Quite amazing, given the tremendous heat of the day and the fact that it scarcely ever rained

On the subject of rations, once every month we would go to a rough and ready store in Dubai to buy some frozen food. The owner had loaned us a chest freezer on the understanding that we would only buy from him. This agreement was easily complied with; his was the only place in town that stocked frozen food! At one time his stock of canned baked beans carried a label depicting a slice of ham on a pile of beans. When our Muslim Messman asked what it was, I explained to him that it was 'Forbidden meat', despite my reassurances that the actual beans he'd eaten had been nowhere near any ham, he scrubbed his tongue with sand!

Dr Kennedy, Al Ain Mission Hospital

About a hundred miles into the desert from our training camp at Manama, there was an experimental agriculture station at Digdugga. It was supervised by a marvelous old Welshman named Morgan. He had been there for about forty years, growing all kinds of garden produce. I never had the opportunity to pay him a visit, but he did come to Manama quite often. We tried to ensure that he enjoyed his visits by wining and dining him as best we could.

Mohammed Saleh, an Arab training officer at Manama, invited me to attend a wedding. The bride's house was in a nearby village. It was a one-roomed, stone building, surrounded by a wall that enclosed about a quarter of an acre of sand.

We joined the main guests, who were all seated on the ground within the room, forming a circle around a large tray on which the food was served.

The meal began with a mysterious, volcanic pile of a porridge-like substance, over which sweet, sticky honey was poured. We ate, of course, with our right hands. This was followed by goat, rice and insipid gravy. As a special treat, cans of fruit were opened and placed on the tray so that we could eat from them with our fingers. Then the host produced a Frankincense Burner.

Each guest took it in turns to cover their heads with their shemaghs in order to allow the heady perfume to penetrate their beards. I did the best I could with my clean shaven chin!

ADDF Browning team on Manama ranges

On a similar occasion; again with Mohammed Saleh, I shook hands with the Mukhtar, or 'head man' of the village, and thanked him for his hospitality. Unfortunately I got my Adeni dialect mixed up with my Gulf, and said,

'Mashkoor, anta lateef katheer, rather than, 'Latheef katheer'

My intention was to thank him for being very kind, but the subtle difference in pronunciation meant that I'd told him he was a sweet homosexual!

The Mukhtar was a big, wild-looking man, with a khunjar (a great, curved dagger) stuck in a bandolier and a beard like a door mat, but he shook with laughter. As for myself, I beat a hasty retreat. As it happens, I was to be involved in another, rather farcical, misinterpretation of meaning.

The time came for my return to the UK. After a lengthy spell of leave, I was posted to the Royal Northumberland Fusiliers at Kirton Lindley in Lincolnshire. I was made welcome by the 'Geordies', whose regiment was due to be amalgamated with the Lancashires. The Regimental Sergeant Major was a real Geordie and a very fine man.

Mulazim (Lieutenant) Abdullah Ali al Baabi, 'A' Squadron, TOS, in 1966
He became a major general in the ADDF

Colonel Edward 'Tug' Wilson, commander of the Abu Dhabi Defence Force

Friday nights in the Northumberland Fusiliers Sergeants' Mess were 'Sod's Opera' nights, conducted by the RSM. Everyone was expected to sing a song or recite some comic verse, etc. Newly arrived, when it came to my turn, I decided to sing 'Poor Jud is dead', from the musical, Oklahoma'.

Unfortunately, the RSM misheard the lyrics and thought I was singing, 'Poor Geordie's dead', as an insulting reference to the regiment's forthcoming demise! With a voice like thunder, he ordered me out of the Mess! It was some time before he accepted an explanation from my friends and allowed me to return to the Mess. Even then, he said that he would go and see the film in order to verify their statements!

Pipers of the ADDF march along the Abu Dhabi cornice in 1971

Editor's note: A previous version of the following account appeared in The Liwa Journal. Summer 2011, edition. Published by the NCDR, Abu Dhabi.

Radio Technicians Ron Wildman and Paddy Wilson checking the power output Of a C13 radio in 1965

9

SPARKS ACROSS ARABIA

Hugh Nicklin Royal Signals

The lumbering RAF Beverley Transport flew low over the blue waters of the Arabian Gulf, heading for Sharjah. It was the 29th of September 1965. Although it was not a long flight from Bahrain, the string bag seat was uncomfortable; a temporary arrangement designed for paratroopers. However, my comfort was not a priority: I was a soldier. I had volunteered for eighteen months service in the desert, seconded from the army to the Foreign Office as a Signaller in an Arab regiment. I was twenty-one and keen to try out anything that looked exciting and different. The Trucial Oman Scouts proved to be exactly that - exciting and very different.

I was greeted by a familiar face, Chas Mitchell, wearing the smart Arab uniform of the TOS, complete with red and white shemagh. The heat here was in complete contrast to the freezing winter we had served together in Lippstadt, Germany. He drove us, in an open top, desert coloured Land Rover, the short distance through the RAF Sharjah camp to the adjoining TOS camp. Here, the tarmac road ran out and we bumped over the sand to a single storey U-shaped accommodation block.

I was to share an air-conditioned four-man room with Chas and two others, Tom Stirzaker and Ron Wildman. We dropped off my bags then went to meet the OC.

Major Morris welcomed me then briefed me on the role of Signallers in the TOS. We, in the Signals Squadron, provided the only means of communication across the whole of Trucial Oman. There were no telephones beyond the camp, and no roads. We also provided a link directly to Bahrain, and from there to the rest of the world. All communication was live traffic and, it is no exaggeration to say, often a matter of life and death. If a vehicle set out from the Base Camp for one of our up-country stations, we needed to have radio confirmation that it had arrived. If it broke down on the way and no one knew about it, with temperatures frequently over 120 degrees, the occupants would soon die of thirst. I was accustomed to handling live traffic. I had used Morse communications every day for six months with the SAS in Borneo. Here, I would be a supervisor. The young Arab operators were very skilled, but, occasionally I would need to man one of the links. On the way to look at the Communications Centre, Chas explained it was not just for messages; it was also a centre for people wanting a lift to outlying stations such as Masafi, Buraimi or Manama. Inside the Comcen, I was greeted with the familiar sound of high pitched Morse code and the crackle of static.

Cpl Chas Mitchell

On a raised area at the back, Arab operators wearing headphones sat at high frequency radio receivers, fingers resting on Morse keys. On one side was the link to Bahrain, on the other the TOS network linking all the outlying TOS camps. There was also a spare position for exercises or whenever another network was needed. The crypto room, where all messages needing encryption and decryption were passed, was visible through a small hatch. Around a corner in another room was the telephone exchange. An Arab operator sat at an old-fashioned switchboard, feverishly answering calls and patching them through. Until recently there had been no connections outside camp, not even a line to Dubai, only five miles away.

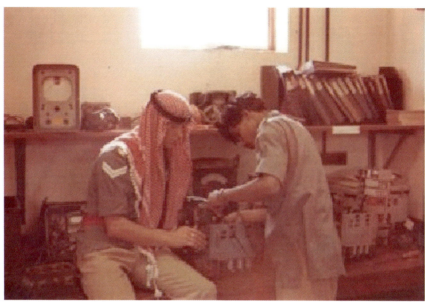
Cpl Ron Wildman in his workshop, training an Arab technician

We next went to meet the Electrician Drivers. There was no mains power outside the base in Sharjah, so all up-country stations had generators, and these were the men who kept them going. In a shed, banks of lead acid batteries were connected to a large charging unit. This was where all the radio batteries were charged up and taken out with the EDs when they went out to maintain the working generators and fix the non-functioning ones.

Our next stop was the radio workshop, where most of the faulty radios were brought in for repair, although some were put back in working order, in situ, by 'Signallers' when they went out on a Maintenance Tour. The radio technicians also looked after the D11 transmitter for the link to Bahrain and the C11 for the TOS network. Our last stop was at the Signals' Quartermaster's Stores, a veritable treasure house of rack upon rack of communications equipment. Clearly we were not short of kit.

That afternoon, I received my uniform of three grey/blue shirts, shemagh, aghul, and a silver Khanjar badge. There were brass badges to go on epaulets and a red lanyard. Footwear consisted of Desert Boots and some tough looking and inflexible sandals; all this with long khaki trousers and a magnificent red stable belt! It was an impressive looking outfit that I couldn't wait to try on. First, though, it was a visit to the camp tailor to have my single, white lance corporal's stripe sewn on. On my first day in the Comcen I found that being a shift worker had its advantages. No parades and no guard duty, although working at weekends and during the night was not so good.

My first job was on the link connecting Sharjah with the JCC in Bahrain, manned mainly by RAF operators, but some Army and Navy too. I put on the earphones, tweaked the RF gain control on the receiver and hit the Morse key.

The next morning, after a salt water shower, I reported to the Comcen again. All was not well. The switchboard operator had gone to the doctor's and, after a cursory explanation,

I was thrust in front of an ancient piece of equipment festooned with a bewildering collection of patch cables, switches and numbered plugholes with an array of small lights; their flashing indicated a call. I had never operated that type of switchboard before, but successfully patched through the first few calls. I was just getting comfortable with the technology when the whole board seemed to light up at once. Try as I might, I couldn't keep up with the urgent requests. The communications room was equally busy, so no help from there. Eventually, Captain Crouch, the 2i/c, arrived to see what was happening. Complaints had been made. He ordered that a more experienced operator should take my place and told me to go and get myself a cup of coffee. Afterwards, he set me the less stressful task of chasing the cable of a faulty telephone extension in the Officers' Mess. He suspected I would find a break or that it had been chewed through by rats.

The Officers' Mess, a large single storey building, was sumptuous compared with our accommodation, which, by army standards, was in itself rather good. The mess servant on duty showed me to a black telephone on a table in the corner. It was, indeed, dead. The connections were intact, so I followed the cable along the skirting board, then through into the next room. From there, it went straight up the wall and disappeared into the ceiling. The mess servant seemed somewhat perplexed by my request for directions on how to get into the roof space, but he eventually showed me to a room with a trap door in the ceiling.

With the help of a chair balanced on top of a table, I scrambled up into a hot and poorly lit space, with a low, corrugated iron roof above me. I had to crawl along a mass of narrow rafters on hands and knees, using the ceiling joists to support my weight. I was soon sweating heavily in the trapped heat of the roof and getting filthy with dust, but I carried on until I found the place where the cable came up. Now I could start to trace it. After thirty feet, I came to a point under the eaves where the roof space was only a foot of clearance. I was now lying on the rafters and holding the cable as I inched forward. Suddenly, a piece of wood beneath my supporting hand broke away and I lost my balance.

I grabbed the rafter, but my legs went through the ceiling. Looking down, I saw I was dangling over a row of cooking pots on a huge stove. Three heads wearing white hats looked up at me in astonishment. I shouted my apologies, lamely explaining I was trying to fix a telephone fault. I became aware of something thrashing me around the legs and hoisted myself back into the roof space. A large brass fan was just below me. As a result of my sudden appearance through the ceiling, it was now swinging left and right as well as going round and round.

Bruised, battered, filthy and exhausted, I cleaned myself up a little before reporting back to Captain Crouch. The news had already reached him and he listened to my account with a mixture of concern and mirth. Whilst observing that it had not been my best day, he took it in good humour. Remembering those open cooking pots, I recommended that he avoid ordering soup for lunch.

Within a month of arriving, I took part in my first up-country exercise, near Manama, up in the mountains. It was to involve the whole regiment and some paratroopers from Bahrain.

After Fred Howley had kitted out our FFR Land Rover with C11 and C42 radios, we set off along the dusty route from Sharjah to Manama. There was no road, just multiple sets of tracks etched into the desert sand. That evening, near Manama camp, we attended a briefing, gathered together between parked Land Rovers and Dodge Power Wagons.

A TOS major and a captain of the Lancers described what was to happen the next day. The paras would be dropping on a DZ, five miles away. They would be followed by an equipment drop, including vehicles and field artillery. The TOS and Lancers would be defending a defined territory against 'invaders' in the form of the 1st Battalion Parachute Regiment. The Lancers, in their Ferret Scout cars, would engage the 'enemy', supporting the TOS. Heavy armour would be provided by the Hussars, travelling from Fujeira, to provide support for the paras. Umpires wearing white armbands would be deployed throughout to keep score.

At dawn the next day we were joined in our Land Rover by a TOS officer, who would be acting as an official observer. Fred and I would provide the communications.

Paratroopers dropping from a Beverley

We lined up at the edge of the Drop Zone, a flat area below the foothills of the Manama mountains, and waited. The sun was climbing high and it was already getting warm. In our open top vehicle we had excellent all-round vision and saw, approaching from the west, two bulbous RAF Beverleys. The side doors were open and, as they lined up for their approach, chutes, like a string of brown mushrooms, filled the sky. The paras landed without casualties. An hour later, the Beverleys reappeared to make the equipment drop. Two platforms bearing lightweight Land Rovers floated down successfully. The third, however, fell far too quickly, the 'chutes only partially deployed. It hit the ground with a thump, breaking its front axle. A write-off, it would take no further part in the exercise.

There were no more serious mishaps, and with the paras and the majority of their equipment safely down, the exercise started in earnest.

That afternoon, battle was joined. As an observer vehicle and considered neutral, we were not targeted. For the next hour, along with the paras, we gradually made our way down the valley. Suddenly, events took a disturbing turn. Live ammunition began ricocheting off the rocks around us. This was supposed to be a simulation, using only blanks and thunder flashes. The exercise was suspended and we were ordered to take cover while everyone tried to work out who was using live ammunition. Eventually, puffs of white smoke were spotted in the surrounding hills. The local tribesmen had seen the parachute drop and had started firing on the invaders. They had no way of knowing this was just an exercise. Fred found a hollow that provided some cover for the Land Rover, and we waited while representatives were sent up into the hills to explain the situation. Eventually, the all-clear message was received from HQ and the exercise resumed. That evening we pulled into a rendezvous point for a debriefing and to cook our evening meal. Action would start again the next day.

Heavy equipment drop. A 'chute has failed to open

Masterchef, Cpl Fred Howley, cooking breakfast

Promptly at 0800, we set off and re-joined the paras who were preparing to advance. Amid the noise of thunder flashes and blanks being fired, came the sound of a powerful diesel engine and, in a cloud of dust, a huge Centurion tank rumbled past us, its gun turret pointed towards the TOS. A cluster of paras hitching a ride on the body of the mighty vehicle, were hanging on like limpets. Later that afternoon a message came through that an air attack was imminent and, as observers, we should rendezvous with the FAC (forward air controller).

A dust-shrouded Centurion tank rumbled past us

We trundled across the desert at the best speed we could manage under the conditions. It was a bumpy ride and the radios shook up and down on their dexion racking. Finally, we drew up beside a lightweight para Land Rover and met the FAC, a cheery captain in the paras. He pointed out a red and yellow T shape made of cloth panels, laid out on the sand and rocks. Half a mile ahead of the T, was the target; a collection of oil drums representing a tank. He explained that the Hunters would fly in on a fixed compass bearing at low level and at a set speed, then pull up, spot the T and the target ahead, then release their rockets. This strategy conferred the element of surprise. A real target wouldn't see or hear the aircraft until the last few seconds.

The FAC's ground to air radio erupted into life and the Hunters announced they were on their way. A minute later, two Mk9 FGA Hunters reared above our heads, with a deafening roar that shook the Land Rover. They dived towards the target and released their rockets. They scored a direct hit, but the oil drums didn't explode as, for the purpose of the exercise, the warheads were made of concrete. They repeated the procedure, using cannon this time, then, with a farewell waggle of their wings, they were gone.

RAF Hawker Hunter FGA 9's about to take off from Sharjah

The exercise drew to a close without further excitement, apart from a thunderflash being thrown into the back of our open Land Rover while I was busy changing frequency on the C11 radio. A thunderflash is a simulated grenade, a giant banger firework, and the explosion nearly blew me out of my seat. My ears were still ringing as we returned to Sharjah

Six months after my arrival in Sharjah, Captain Dykins, the education officer, organised a camel patrol over the Easter break; the purpose being to check the names and positions of the more remote wells. On the existing maps, four of them were named in the Arabic for, 'I Don't Know!'

We set off early on the Friday morning. The Bedford three ton truck lurched and bumped along the desert track, while the five of us who had volunteered, sat in the back and watched the scenery pass by. At around noon we drew up at our destination, a collection of Bedu tents and barusti huts in the middle of nowhere. Captain Dykins told us we were guests in a Bedouin village and were expected to attend a ceremonial meal with the tribal elders.

The village headman approached us with a welcoming smile. Followed by an entourage of Bedu warriors, he exuded an air of great authority and wore a magnificent red headdress.

After the usual greetings and responses, we were led to a barusti shelter where huge circular brass platters were set out on carpets. We washed our hands in a basin arrangement at the edge and were ushered in to sit down. I was seated with Captain Dykins, Charles Pirie, the headman and two of his tribesmen. Captain Dykins conversed with the headman in fluent Arabic. Although I did not fully understand what they were talking about, their conversation seemed to be about his tribe; the logistics of the forthcoming camel patrol and the territory we would be covering. At a signal, servants came in carrying steaming cauldrons of rice and mildly curried vegetables. The rice was piled in the centre of the platter and the vegetables spread around the edge. A pot containing the meat was brought in and the contents spread on top of the rice. It was difficult to tell if it was goat or sheep, but it was delicious. Mint tea followed, served in tiny, delicate china cups. When everything was cleared away, the headman stood up and produced a tiny glass phial. Using a feather, he took a few drops of the perfume and stroked it on the wrist of each of us in turn, speaking a few words of blessing for our journey.

The hospitable village headman

It was then time to meet the camels. None of us had ridden before and the saddles looked a long way up! The camel driver, dressed in white with a white shemagh, made some guttural noises and hissing sounds and the beasts immediately folded their legs and sat down. Captain Dykins translated some brief instructions, then mounted his own camel. I followed suit. There wasn't much of a saddle and no stirrups or reins, only a short length of rope. I clung on as I was thrown forward when the back legs stood up then backwards as the front ones stood. When we were all aboard, the leader, made a guttural sound and his steed strode forward.

The rest of us followed. Occasionally, my camel would bend forward to take a bite of vegetation, usually prickly camel thorn. It's amazing to me that something so tough could be digested at all.

Around mid-afternoon, I sensed a change of mood in my camel, a quickening of pace and a sense of urgency. The rest of the camels also speeded up. After another mile, a well came into view. We filled our water carriers and set off again. Two more hours and our guide called a halt for the day. The trip was being catered by the cameleers and they set to work preparing an evening meal that smelled rather good.

The days fell into a pattern. We filled our water bottles before setting off each morning and dropped in two pills. One was to kill the bugs and stank of chlorine. The other was to disguise the taste of the first. Some of the wells we passed were shared by livestock, so it was wise to take precautions. As it transpired, despite our precautions, my good friend, Chas Pirie contracted dysentery and had to be taken to Manama. See his account in this book.

At breakfast we drank chai; sweet black tea flavoured with mint. In the evenings, we were served the most delicious Arab coffee laced with cardamoms, poured from a brass coffee pot blackened by the fire. No sugar, no milk, just pure aromatic coffee made from freshly ground beans.

Me aboard my trusty steed

We came across a large, wild, lactating camel which our guides chased and caught then proceeded to milk. They brought us a large bowl of fresh camel's milk and urged us to try some. It was warm and creamy, with a strong flavour. Our guides considered it to be a real treat.

Lying in my sleeping bag looking up at the night sky was a wonderful experience. I had never seen so many stars and felt as though I was falling upwards into a sea of lights. The only sound to be heard was that of our camels moving around in the semi darkness.

One evening we witnessed an extraordinary display of skill by Captain Dykins. Our Bedu guides had produced a pair of live chickens, which they had kept in a wickerwork cage aboard the luggage camel.

' Do you know how to hypnotise a chicken,' he asked us. We shook our heads.

Reaching across he took hold of one of the chickens from our guide, put it down on the sand, and while it squawked and clucked in protest, he pressed its head downwards. He slowly drew a line in the sand with his finger starting at the bird's beak. Its eyes crossed following the finger while the rest of it remained absolutely inert. Captain Dykins then stood up and we all looked down at a completely comatose bird. Amazing! It was so quick and the effect so remarkable we were dumbstruck. Even our guide was impressed as he had never seen anything quite like it either.

'I grew up on a farm', said the captain, 'and we used to do this to check if they were egg bound. Quickly put them out for the count, then stick your finger up the rear end to check.'

Capt Dykins, Paddy Wilson, Chas Pirie, our guide and Jim Rayment

There is a peculiar rhythm and pace on a camel that appears slow and relaxed, but actually covers a lot of ground surprisingly quickly. Our mission to identify the correct names of the wells was not meeting with much success. So far, we had only found two of the un-named ones.

The Arabs we encountered all said they didn't know anything about the wells. So we plodded on in the hope that we would eventually meet someone who did. That was fine as far as I was concerned.

I enjoyed the whole experience and came to understand why, for thousands of years, that unique animal, the camel, had been the only means of transport that could traverse such an inhospitable and arid wasteland.

July was probably the hottest time of the year, with temperatures of over 120 degrees F, but I had persuaded Sergeant Major Ash to allow me to go on Tech Tour with the radio technician and electrician drivers in order to familiarise myself with the outlying stations.

With our Bedford truck loaded with spares and enough food for a fortnight, we set off at dawn heading for Manama. Our crew consisted of Steve Cartwright, the radio tech, Mick Wilson, the ED, Said Ahmed, an Arab ED, and myself.

Manama is located in the foothills of the range that separated Trucial Oman from the Sultanate of Oman. It is a dry and rocky environment and was our main infantry training area. Our accommodation was in tents which didn't have air-conditioning but, fortunately, the nights were a little cooler here inland where there was less humidity.

Bursting through the palm trees at Buraimi Oasis

The next day Mick and Said Ahmed were kept busy servicing the generators that provided the power for the radios in the camp. Steve checked the radio equipment, but had little to do except replace a faulty headset. Another dawn start and our three-tonner headed south, along the dusty track towards Buraimi.

After the washed out colours of the desert, driving into the oasis was a complete contrast, with the dark green of the palm trees, green grass and crops of vegetables growing in small fields. It was busier, too, with people going about their daily business, herding sheep, goats, donkeys and camels.

Jahili fort in Al Ain was quite stunning to look at; it stood brilliant white against the cloudless blue sky.

Steve Cartwright and Mick Wilson outside Ft. Jahili

After a few days spent checking out the generators, the battery store, and repairing a faulty C13 radio, it was time to move on to Abu Dhabi. A problem with one of the power generators delayed our start, so the air temperature was well over 100 degrees in the shade by the time we set off. By 1230, steam was issuing from the bonnet of the Bedford. Half an hour later, it was boiling like a kettle. Our only recourse was to drive it to the top of a dune, point it into the wind and allow it to cool down. At 1500, we set off once again, keeping a close eye on the temperature gauge. Abu Dhabi came into view a little before sundown.

The Sheik's palace was impressive, but the rest of the town was simply a collection of primitive buildings and barusti huts; light years away from the mass of skyscrapers, port facilities, shopping malls and green spaces it would become in little more than two decades.

We had to report to the British Political Agent. He was the Foreign Office's representative. His residence was one of the few buildings that looked in good order. We made ourselves as comfortable as possible, spending the night in a building that served as temporary accommodation for visitors.

The following morning we visited the Corniche to see the international banks that overlooked the harbour.

An early sign of world interest in the region, the five structures, enormous by the standards of the time and built out of imported stone, marble and glass, looked very impressive and quite out of keeping with their surroundings.

After the usual checking and repairing of equipment, our next stop would be Mirfa. On the way, we crossed the famous water pipeline the Sheikh had built, bringing water in from the jebel. `A group of Bedus were watering their goats and camels.

We waited until they had finished, then took the opportunity to fill our jerry cans. It was going to be another long, hot trek across sabkah and desert before we reached the camp at Mirfa.

A young Bedu lad, filled with curiosity, came over to have a chat with us and have his photograph taken.

The ruler of Abu Dhabi's palace in July 1966

We arrived at Mirfa in late afternoon. The TOS camp, a tented arrangement, was on the beach, many miles from anywhere. It was very hot and unbelievably humid. This was not surprising as the sabkha, or salt flats, stretched for miles. The sea was very shallow here and prone to a high level of evaporation. How the resident Squadron coped with this for three months of the summer, with virtually no air-conditioning was beyond me. There would be work for me to do here. With the climate and the salt content in the air, there were always things to be fixed. Even though the radios were, supposedly, hermetically sealed, they were still prone to corrosion in such an atmosphere. The next morning, Steve Cartwright examined the maintenance log of the Squadron's radios and checked what needed to be done. While we removed corrosion, identified and replaced faulty valves, Mick Wilson and Said sorted out the generators. Eventually, the job was done, the generators were serviced and battery packs topped up. We set off once again, heading along the coast to Sharjah

At the pipeline, Mick Wilson, a bedu lad, our driver, Said Ahmed, and Steve Cartwright

Mirfa, the camp on the beach. Very hot and humid

. In the summer months it could be navigated with ease, but come winter, with a little rain or an especially high tide, the hard sabkah would be transformed into treacherous quicksand. Many a vehicle became bogged down by skirting too close to the sea and sinking up to their axles- or deeper. The previous winter, Mick had helped pull out a truck that was being used on an exercise from Bahrain. Happily, we made our journey, without incident.

Hugh Nicklin

10

DANCES, DJs AND DYSENTERY

Charles Pirie Royal Signals

'Good morning, sir. Your early wake up call, here's a cup of tea. Breakfast is in twenty minutes. You need to be in the main departure area for 7am, ready for your VC10 flight to Bahrain.'
 I had spent the night in the transit block at RAF Lyneham. It all came back to me. Three months ago, while I was attached to the 69 Field Squadron Royal Engineers in Hamelin, Germany, as corporal in charge of a small signal troop providing communications for the field Squadron, I had seen on the Squadron's notice board that the Foreign Office were looking for volunteers (all trades) to serve in the Trucial Oman Scouts in Trucial Oman. It had been a lovely summer in Germany but, having survived three German winters, I was not looking forward to another one. I love the sun and here was a chance to serve in one of the hottest places on earth. I sent off my application and was accepted. Now here I was, about to board the VC10 which would, as it turned out, be the first stage of a journey to where I would enjoy the best two years of my army service. Two years I would always think back to with fond memories.

Beverley

We landed in Bahrain and disembarked. I spent the night in the RAF transit camp at Manama then boarded a Beverley transport plane up to Sharjah. I had never seen a Beverley before, so this large 'plane with its cavernous belly and apparently nowhere to carry passengers, was a sight to see. Upon asking a loader where I would be sitting he pointed to a ladder attached to the side of the plane which disappeared through a circular hole cut into one of the twin booms sticking out the rear of the plane.

'Up there, mate', he said with a smile when he saw my face. 'It's okay there are plenty of seats and some portholes you can look out of.'

We flew at around 5,000 feet, with the clear blue waters of the gulf showing shoals and reefs below us. Sandy shallows reflected the strong sunlight. In what seemed like no time at all we were on our glide path to Sharjah.

The heat struck me like a hammer blow when I got off that 'plane; it must have been in excess of 40c. Oh well, I thought, this is what I came for and, lo and behold, here it is.

Before I managed to gather up my kit, a lanky guy, languidly smoking a cigarette in a long holder, came over and asked if I was Charles Pirie.

'That's me', I said.

He introduced himself as Fred Howley. 'This is my Land Rover. Jump in. I'll take you down to our lines and get you settled in.'

The next morning, after breakfast, it was off to the stores to get my TOS uniform. Fred showed me how to wear my shemagh, pointing out that the blue musree shirt was worn over the trousers and not tucked in. He then gave me a tour of the laundry, the camp barber shop, the tailors, the Scouts Club, and to my delight, introduced me to our batman. Fred explained that he would look after my kit, take care of my dhobi and keep my room clean, even making my bed for me! I thought to myself, this is some sort of corporals' heaven.

After morning break, I was introduced to WO2 Tim Ash at Signals HQ. He explained what I would be doing and what was expected of me, he took me in to see the man in charge, Major Morris. He welcomed me to the Squadron and gave me an oversight of the Trucial Oman Scouts, and, more specifically, the role of the signals team in the grand scheme of things.

My job, when in camp, was to be a supervisor in the communications centre. It had a direct link to the one at the Joint Services in Bahrain. We controlled the radio network which connected the various Squadrons established all over the Trucial States.

We had a 'secure room' where traffic was encrypted or decrypted by a corporal cypher operator; for most of my time with the TOS this was a great guy called Dick Viner. When a major exercise was planned, I was usually relieved of duty in the comcen and given a Land Rover fitted with a radio. Attached to HQ, I provided radio communications between the Squadrons on exercise out in the desert.

Our batman, Ali

On one occasion, during such an exercise, a very worried Colonel Freddie de Butts, the TOS commander at the time, came onto the net, requesting immediate help. His vehicle was bogged down on a beach and the tide was rising. By the time help arrived, the Land Rover was submerged to the top of the doors. It was eventually retrieved by a recovery vehicle when the tide went out again.

For the rest of the year things carried on much as normal, working shifts in the communications centre, off duty trips down to Sharjah Creek for fishing, snorkeling, swimming and sunbathing. A local man, who lived on the other side of the creek, had a barusti hut on the side we used. As soon as he saw us, he would jump into a rowing boat, come over and open it up. Inside, among other things, was a kerosene operated refrigerator stacked with our favourite cans of soft drinks. He was quite an enterprising chap; between the TOS, the RAF and the British armoured Squadrons that used to come to Sharjah for desert training, I am sure he made a living wage for himself and his family.

Shortly after Christmas 1965, our 2IC Captain Tripp had a nasty accident.

He had driven to Dubai during daylight, but darkness had fallen by the time he began the return journey to Sharjah. His Land Rover nose-dived into a large hole in the track, causing him life threatening injuries. He was casevaced back to the UK where I believe, he eventually made a full recovery. His replacement was Captain Crouch, a very good officer who we will meet again, later in this narrative.

Oooops!

New Year celebrations were held in the 'Scouts Club', where the junior NCOs did their socializing. In our opinion it was the best 'Mess' in the camp. The buffet our corporal chef put on for us when we had a 'do' was second to none. The food and the manner in which he presented it was worthy of five stars. The officers tried to lure him to their mess, but, apart from helping them out with the Annual TOS Ball, he stayed with us.

The Ball was themed, and the first time I acted as one of its waiters, the Officers' Mess had been transformed into a sheikh's tent. Its walls were draped with fabric and the floor covered with cushions and low tables set out. The guests were all beautiful young ladies, flown in by the RAF from all over the globe; the officers having vacated their rooms to provide them with accommodation. Unfortunately, us volunteer waiters could only observe the 'goings on'. We would have gladly paid good money to join in!

The following year, the Officers' Mess was transformed into a London Underground platform. Corrugated iron was put up to make the place look like a tunnel. It was very well done. The ball, which attracted a lot of 'socialites', was even reported in the Daily Express. If our corporal chef and the officer who themed the mess had got together in 'civvy street', they would have probably made a fortune.

There was a radio station on the RAF camp called Forces Radio Sharjah.

Some members of the TOS used to help out with the broadcasts; a friend of mine, Ron Wildman, did a few shifts as sound engineer. One night, as we were having a few drinks together in the Scouts Club, I told him that I didn't think much to the way the programmes were presented, to which he replied,

'Well, if you think you can do better I'll put you up for an interview with the station boss.'

Me and my big mouth! I couldn't back down, so a few days later I was shown into the boss's office, an RAF Warrant Officer, who greeted me with,

'So, you want to produce and present programmes, do you?'

After a chat about the kind of programme I wanted to produce and present, he took me into a small sound studio and handed me a copy of an old UK shipping forecast bulletin.

Relaxing on Sharjah Creek

'Read that', he said, 'and we'll find out how you sound on air'.

Those who have heard the shipping forecast will know it takes around 10 minutes and includes a few 'tongue twisters'. I finished reading it without too many mispronunciations and then he played it back. I have never liked the sound of my own voice, but after he had listened to my efforts, he said,

'Excellent, when do you want to start?'

Ron showed me how to use the sound equipment on the console in the sound-proof studio where I would be presenting my folk music in a programme which I called 'Hootenanny'. I worked there for the next 12 months or so and eventually had my own folk, Latin American and request programmes. Not long after I started doing requests, Captain Crouch asked me not to accept those satirical choices that were asked for when an officer or senior NCO had made a 'horlicks' of something.

Life went on fairly smoothly for the next few months. Easter was approaching and word went out that they were looking for volunteers to mount a camel patrol over the holiday. Another friend, Neddy Nicklin, always seemed to find out about these things before anyone else, so I was one of the first to sign up. The leader of the five-man patrol was Captain Dykins. We were meeting up at the village whose head man was supplying us with camels and three guides. Our task was to navigate to five wells that had been surveyed ten or more years earlier by a Royal Engineers survey team. They had asked their guides the names of each well and marked them on their maps. Their guides didn't have names for them, so their Arabic replies to the engineers were, 'No idea' or 'Haven't a clue'.

We were tasked to find out the names of the wells, or at least the names of their locations, so that new maps would be up to date.

Donkey Derby on Christmas Day 1965

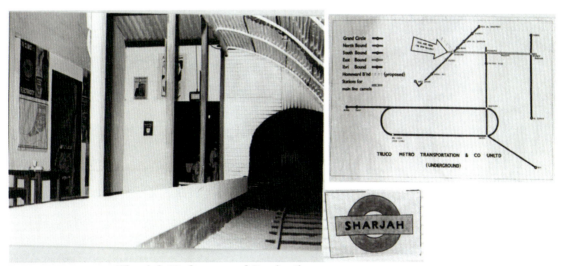
'Sharjah Underground Station!'

When we arrived at the village we were introduced to our guides by our host, the village head man, and our guides introduced us to our mounts, which we would be spending the next five days with.

Once the usual pleasantries had been exchanged, we were shown how to mount our camel, how to make it get up, bear left or right, and how to make it kneel down so we could dismount. We then set off with our camels roped together.

Our cameleers kept a close eye on us as we wended our way round the sand dunes and across a gravel plain.

We stopped for a break and were told that we seemed to be managing so well we would now be in control of our own camel. That was fine by us, but after we had travelled across the plain for several miles, our camels, without warning, broke into a gallop. Now a galloping camel is not a bit like a galloping horse. It isn't called the ship of the desert for nothing. It moves forward with the left back leg and the left front leg going in opposite directions and its right legs following suit. The ungainly beast sways from side to side like a ship in a heavy sea -- most unpleasant. We all managed to stay mounted, except for Paddy Wilson who took fright and leapt off his camel's back, then watched it charge off into the distance. The camels had smelled water from the first well we were visiting, sniffing it out while we were still about half a mile from it.

Twenty minutes later, Paddy Wilson arrived on foot. He was hot and dusty, but still in one piece. He had to put up with quite a slagging from the rest of us for abandoning his camel.
We drank water from the same source as the camels, after we'd added chlorine tablets to it, adding another tablet that improved the taste somewhat. It was just about drinkable and that was that.

On the second day, one of our guides spotted a camel with a young one and took off after them. A short time later he returned with a large pan of camel's milk, still warm, which he handed round. We all took a good drink. It had a fairly strong flavour, but was still quite a pleasant drink. The temperatures we were experiencing at mid-day would have been in the low to mid forties Celsius. Our only protection from the sun was the shemaghs covering our heads and shoulders.
On the morning of the third day, I was starting to feel quite ill and, by mid morning I was experiencing serious diarrhoea. By the afternoon I was in a bad way; losing all the water I was drinking, almost immediately, I was rapidly dehydrating.

Chas Pirie on his camel

   As a consequence, I began to suffer from heatstroke and my temperature was rising fast. We had no radio with us and were still about a day's journey from the nearest track where we might encounter TOS vehicles on their way to Manama or Sharjah.
   Captain Dykins saved my life; keeping me hydrated by making me drink salt water. We spent another night in the desert. Without the heat of the sun to trouble me and with all the water I needed, my temperature dropped a little.

   It was decided we had to make an early start to get to the vehicle track. We found it, right where we expected it to be and it wasn't long before I was lying in the back of a three ton Bedford truck on its way to Manama, where there were some basic medical facilities.

   For the next two days I lay on a bed in the medic marquee with two electric fans blowing cool air at me and an unlimited supply of water to drink. My temperature had been 103 F when I arrived in Manama, but it had gone below 100 before I was transferred by Land Rover to the RAF hospital in Sharjah. I was diagnosed with dysentery and fed copious amounts of tetracycline to kill the nasty bug that caused it. Five days later and two stone lighter, I was discharged fit and well and thanking my lucky stars I was still alive to tell the tale.

Coffee Time. Grinding up the beans with a mortar and pestle

11

CHAS PIRIE SHOWS THE FLAG

As reported to Hugh Nicklin

The Dodge Power Wagon pulled up outside our accommodation block a little after 1130, and the Arab duty driver knocked on the blue door of Chas Pirie's room.

Hastily pulling on some shorts, Chas glanced out of the window, thinking, I'm not on shift today, what's he doing here?

'Corporal Pirie, sahib, Captain Crouch say you come now to office.'

'What the heck does the 2 i/c Signals want with me? It's my day off.

'OK Sohail. Five minutes –tamaam?'

The driver nodded and went back to his DPW. Chas rushed down to the washrooms for a splash and shave doing his best to look presentable. He muttered to himself, 'I'm not putting uniform on just for half an hour,' as he dressed in clean civilian clothes.

Captain Crouch's door was already open when Chas arrived.

'Come in Corporal Pirie. 'Sorry to drag you in on your day off, but I need to talk to you. Please shut the door and take a seat.'

This is mighty cordial, thought Chas. I know he's from Edinburgh too, but he is an officer and I'm a junior NCO. There's something important going on here, and they want me to say yes to it. 'You know the QDGs are the resident armoured Squadron?'

Chas nodded. 'Yes, sir, but I've had very little to do with them.'

'Well, you are going to have a lot more to do with them soon.'

'But, sir, I don't want to leave the TOS.'

'Relax, corporal. This is a short term assignment. You'll be back with us in no time at all. Ever been to Muscat?'

'No, sir, that's not part of the Trucial Oman.'

'Indeed it isn't, and it's usually outside of our jurisdiction.'

Captain Crouch went on to explain that the level of unrest in neighbouring Aden was getting worse. Also the number of insurgents crossing the border and stirring up trouble in Oman and Muscat was growing. It was causing concern in Whitehall and the Foreign Office, and the Sultan was becoming uneasy. They didn't want a repeat of the Jebel Ahkdar campaign of seven years ago. As a consequence of all this, LFPG (Land Forces Persian Gulf) had decided it was time for a spot of sabre rattling. The Sultan's Armed Forces didn't have any armour, so, we would make a show of strength to dissuade any dissidents from trying their luck. The Queen's Dragoon Guards would be sending a Squadron on a tour of Muscat and Oman in their Ferret armoured cars. Chas would accompany them in a FFR (Fitted For Radio) Land Rover. His job would be to provide radio links back to here and whatever long range links they might require.

Although the QDG had their own radios and Signallers, they did tactical inter-squadron communications and, perhaps, work with infantry, but they didn't know how to break into the TOS network or work with Arab operators. They had specifically requested TOS support. Chas would
be the link back to Sharjah and then back to LFPG Bahrain. He would be using a QDG Land Rover and would need to dress like the British Army in order to blend in. The QDG stores would provide everything – even a Jimmy cap badge. It was thought that the sight of a red and white shemagh in a military vehicle swanning around in Muscat, would cause a stir, and be something the locals would notice. They might interpret it as the Trucial Oman muscling in on their territory. That would be just the kind of thing to make trouble in such a sensitive area. It's seen as acceptable for them to have a British Army presence, but not a military outfit from a neighbouring country. The SAF wore blue and white shemaghs, and Chas would be guests of the SAF and the Muscat Gendarmerie, who would look after and accompany him.

'All righ, sir.' I understand. 'When do we go?'

'Monday. Take yourself off to the QDG's tomorrow morning at 0900 and pick up your kit. Ask for Lieutenant Jenkin. He's expecting you and he'll show you around.'

'You're looking surprisingly spruce for someone on their day off. Got yourself a date, have you?' I said, as I walked up to Chas in the cookhouse queue.

'Oh, hi, Neddy. No, the only dates in this place are the ones that grow on palm trees.' He was grinning, so I knew something was up.

'Crouchie just told me that I'm off to Muscat for a couple of weeks with the QDG. I've got to wear their blue beret and KD (kakhi drill). No TOS shemaghs allowed.'

'Fantastic! I've always wanted to see Muscat and Oman. They have huge mountains, and it's quite lush in places, apparently. But according to some of the SAS guys I know, the 20th century hasn't reached there yet. They were involved in the Jebel Akhdar campaign. They climbed that 10,000 ft peak in the middle of the night and surprised the rebels, who hid in a cave and had to be flushed out with a bazooka. A lot of people forget that the TOS were involved in that battle too, as well as the SAF.'

'Well, we're going in Ferrets and Land Rovers, Neddy, so I hope they have some petrol up there. I'm not too happy about wearing a British Army uniform again.'

A modern map of the region: Trucial Oman is now the UAE

Early on a Monday morning, the sheepish-looking Corporal Chas Pirie, Royal Corps of Signals, emerged from his room dressed in khaki drill and blue beret. He was about to climb into a waiting Land Rover when our little sending-off committee of Trucial Oman Scout well-wishers erupted into wolf whistles and jeers.

'Sod off you lot! Bloody well go back to bed. Can't you see I'm going on an important mission!?'

That got everyone laughing as Chas sped off across the sand, passed the NAAFI and went out of sight. The first stop on the journey was Buraimi, with its characteristic white fort nicknamed 'The Wedding Cake'. The stream of desert-camouflaged Ferret armoured cars and a few Land Rovers made an impressive sight against the backdrop of this old fort.

*'A' Squadron Queen's Dragoon Guards lined up
In their Ferrets and ready to go.*

Chas sat in the passenger seat of his FFR Land Rover, along with a driver from the QDG. A C11 HF radio in the back was to be the Squadron's only link with the outside world. The OC, a young Lieutenant, strode over from his Ferret.

'How are you settling in corporal, everything fine?'

'Yes sir,' said Chas, 'everyone's made me feel most welcome.'

'That's good, because you are welcome, corporal. We're pleased to have you provide us with a link back home. You were not present at the briefing, so I'll give you the advice we received. You're obviously familiar with this area and the relative do's and don'ts, but we are about to enter an altogether different country. Muscat and Oman is still stuck in the Middle Ages. The old sultan forbids education or any involvement with the modern world. It is very much a closed country. You could transport people from 1,000 years ago, put them there and they would feel right at home. Their daily life would be exactly the same.' He leaned forward. 'As you've probably been told, there's been an increase in the number of insurgents sneaking across the Yemeni border and aiding the rebel gangs. We are here to show the flag on our little tour. The message the Sultan wants to send out is, 'Don't mess with me because I've got powerful friends. We don't expect much trouble, but there's always the possibility that we will get shot at. Some chaps up in the hills will happily bang away with their old Martini-Henry rifles when they feel like it – we can expect a few pot shots – but nothing to worry about. So be prepared and be watchful.'

It's all right for you, mate, thought Chas, you're in a Ferret with an inch of Chobham armour. I'm in a SSV (soft skinned vehicle) Land Rover, with nothing, but a flimsy bit of canvas for protection!

'OK sir. I'll be careful,' replied Chas, feeling a sense of grim foreboding as he gazed towards the mountains and the border.

To take his mind off his feelings, Chas erected a longer whip aerial, connected it to his C11 radio and turned on the set. The shorter travelling aerial would not transmit as much power as a longer one in the HF band.

The ideal aerial would be a long wire dipole strung between two masts and cut to half the wavelength of the frequency, but with no convenient trees around and no 30 ft. telescopic masts in his Land Rover, he made the best of what he had. Turning the coffee grinder handle on the ATU, he did his best to match the aerial and get the dial up to maximum power. Sitting in the back of his Land Rover, with the Morse key on his knee, he tapped out a Sitrep (situation report) back to Sharjah, informing them that they had arrived in Buraimi and would cross the border into Oman the following morning.

The evening meal was a cheerful affair; everyone being very friendly and welcoming. Chas had the slightly surreal feeling that he had been invited along on a family motoring trip rather than a potentially life-threatening patrol into enemy territory. The QDG are a long established and very senior cavalry regiment, second only to the Blues and Royals in the British Army's pecking order. Generations of soldiers recruited from the border region of Wales and England have served with the regiment since its inception. It is also known as the Welsh Cavalry. As with many other regiments, tradition is a key element. This is quite different from serving in the Royal Signals, thought Chas, we're the new kids on the block, formed out of the Royal Engineers between the two world wars. We don't travel around together as one big family. It's mix and match for us. A posting here and then another there, we rarely stay with the same group for very long. Unlike these regimental types and we're always having to make new friends. Lots of variety, but none of the family continuity these guys enjoy.

A border outpost manned by members of the Sultan's Armed Forces

The following morning they headed for the mountains and the Muscat Oman border. When they reached it, Chas felt a level of unease as he gazed up into the mountains beyond the checkpoint. A couple of guards dressed in blue and white shemaghs and armed with 303in rifles, smiled and waved them through. They had obviously been expected.

The track was narrow and twisting, with massive cliffs on either side. This is just perfect for an ambush, Chas thought. There were no roads as such, just stony tracks and not a single inch of tarmac. The going was slow and the scenery dramatic.

After an hour or so, Chas relaxed a little. Nobody had taken a pot shot at them, and the few locals they passed had waved in a friendly manner. Perhaps things would be fine in his Land Rover without armour plate. He had the window open, allowing the mountain breeze to cool his face. Those Ferret armoured cars gave a hot and noisy ride; this was so much better.Some hours later, the scenery became less dramatic as they left the hill country behind them. Low buildings started to appear and there were people grazing their animals. Ahead of them the beginnings of a town came into view.

Emerging from a wadi en route to Nizwa. Note Chas' desert boot in

'I think this is it for the night, boyo.' said Chas' driver in a strong Welsh accent. He pulled up next to a Ferret and opened his door. 'I'd better go see the OC. He might want the radio near to him; I'll be back in a jiffy.'

Chas got out, stretched, and looked around at the place. Other than their own little convoy, there were no vehicles to be seen. The donkey was the main mode of transport and king of the road out here. There were few shops and no advertising hoardings. Herds of goats were wandering around as though they owned the place, mixing in with a few camels.

Stray dogs were barking at these odd-looking newcomers and a group of ragged-looking children gazed at them with a mixture of curiosity and caution. It all looked dusty and flyblown. There's probably no electricity either, thought Chas. Yep! It looks like something from the middle- ages, all right.

His driver was back again.

'This place is called Ibri -- the boss says. He wants the radio next to his Ferret, over there. He's writing out a message for you to send to Sharjah, now.'

Resting outside the walls of Nizwa.

Once the vehicle was parked, Chas erected the longest whip aerial he had, climbed in the back, turned on the C11 and tuned it in to the TOS network frequency. The Morse code message was quickly transmitted.

The Lieutenant watched Chas in action on the Morse key.

'Anything for us, corporal?'

'No sir, no messages.'

'We might as well pack it up until tomorrow, then. It'll give you a chance to get yourself organised for the night. There's only an hour of daylight left.'

'How long are we staying here, sir?'

'Only tonight, then we go on to Nizwa. It's a much larger place than this. We'll stay there for a few days. We'll end up at the capital, Muscat City, via a place called Bidbid.' The lieutenant laughed, 'great name isn't it? What do you think of Muscat and Oman so far?'

'Great scenery, sir, but as you said, it's quite mediaeval. It really is like stepping back several hundred years.'

The lieutenant smiled and nodded, 'I'd better go and sort out a couple of things, too. Would you care to join us for an after dinner drink corporal?'

'Well, thank you, sir, I would.'

He's probably about the same age as me, thought Chas; in his early twenties and only a couple of years out of Sandhurst. I seem to have been in the army forever and I'm only 23, but then I did start at the Army Apprentice College in Harrogate when I was fifteen.

'A camel through the eye of a needle': the gateway into fortified Nizwa

The cooks were busy in their field kitchen. They managed to turn out a wholesome and tasty meal from a mixture of composite rations and fresh produce. Chas queued up with the Dragoons, their lilting Welsh voices and lively banter made him feel like a welcome guest.

The following morning, the line of Ferret scout cars and Land Rover support vehicles, drove out of Ibri, heading for Nizwa. They passed through wadis and a few fields of cultivation. Rainfall was higher here than in Trucial Oman. As the Lieutenant had said, Nizwa was an altogether bigger place. It had some large, stone built government buildings and it was fortified with a high surrounding wall. Doubtless it had seen some action in the past.

At the outskirts, they came across a camel train resting under whatever shade they could find.

'A' Squadron pulled up outside the walls and set up camp. The only way into the town was through an ancient, narrow gateway, which was high enough for a camel to pass through, but not for a vehicle. The place appeared to exist in a time warp.

Nizwa in the 1960's. A town still living in the

The Bottle Dungeon in Nizwa. The prisoner down below is fed through a hole.

A captain, dressed in the red beret of the Muscat Gendarmerie, part of the Sultans Armed Forces, came out to meet them with a troop of guards. He had taken up a position in the SAF after leaving the British army. This was not unusual as the SAF usually recruited its senior NCOs and officers this way. He addressed the Squadron.

'Gentleman, on behalf of His Majesty, the Sultan of Oman and Muscat, may I bid you a most sincere welcome to his country. He is most grateful for this show of strength by his friends, the British, and particularly yourselves -- The Queen's Dragoon Guards. He hopes your stay will be an enjoyable one. As you know, this is a closed country, untouched by much of the modern world. A few words of warning which I hope you'll keep in mind as you travel through Muscat and Oman. Here in Nizwa, and in other towns, there is a curfew at sundown. At that time, the gates to the town are shut and nobody can enter or leave until dawn the following morning. There's nothing like street lighting or electricity here in Nizwa, or anywhere, except Muscat City itself. Most people stay in their houses at night. Anyone out and about after sundown has to carry a lighted lamp. Failure to do so will result in that person being arrested, and occasionally someone gets shot, because they are considered to be up to no good if they haven't got a lantern.'

He paused to let that sink in as some worried glances were exchanged between some members of his audience. 'So be aware. Do not wander around on your own after dark. Anyway, there's nothing to see and nowhere much to go. During the day, you can go pretty much wherever you like. It's extremely safe here, and there's very little crime. You will be made welcome, and treated with respect by the locals. Obviously we expect you to do the same. Remember you are all ambassadors for Britain.'

The ramparts of Nizwa-the cannon in the embrasures were loaded!

*View across the harbour from the gun battery at
the top of Muscat's fortifications.*

Chas sent his usual evening Sitrep message to Sharjah, and once again there were no messages to receive. This is easy work, he thought; less than an hour a day. I suppose this place must be something like it was in Britain, a long time ago. He felt like a time traveller. Shades of HG Wells; my Land Rover is a 'Time Machine.'

'Corporal Pirie,' it was the OC. 'Any messages for us this evening?'

'No, sir, nothing. I was just thinking how we appear to be travelling into the past.'

'Yes, it does feel a bit like that,' He paused for a moment, as if remembering something, 'Tomorrow, the Captain's kindly offered to give me and the Sergeant a guided tour of Nizwa. Would you care to come along?'

'Yes, sir, I would like that very much. Thank you.'

The following morning, the Gendarmerie Captain appeared, smiling and smart in his starched khaki uniform. He took them on a tour of the fortified town, along the ramparts and gun positions and through the narrow winding streets to the tower, with its commanding view over the surrounding countryside. Any potential attacker would be seen long before they approached the walls, and the large, strategically placed cannons, would dispatch them in short order.

'The last place I want to show you are the dungeons', the captain told them.

That sounds interesting, thought Chas. It'll probably be something like an old castle in the UK; an empty chamber to show tourists around.

Armed tribesmen about to parley with the Sultan.

Their little party moved on to the dungeon. The captain hardly had to indicate the place.

'Here we are, just down there. See where those chaps are lifting off that cover.' They peered into the gloom of an underground vault. With bars across the opening, there was a tiny hole about a foot in diameter. The stench was awful. The captain continued his tourist spiel, 'It's a bottle dungeon. The chap in there is chained up, so he's not going anywhere. There's not much room, so he can't really stand up properly, either. The only way in is through this hole, and he was lowered into it a couple of years ago. His family come and feed him though the bars every day.'

There was a sound of scuffling and whimpering from below. The smell, if anything, was getting worse. Chas felt sick, his stomach heaved as he tried to keep down whatever wanted to come up.

Bidbid was similar to Ibri, a collection of low buildings and the same signs of a rural subsistence lifestyle. They spent a night there, then travelled on to Muscat, the capital – a fortified city with a magnificent harbour. The Ferrets and Land Rovers pulled up outside the high city walls.

'Wow,' said Chas to his driver, 'just look at that! It's like some Knights of the Round Table castle.'

'Yeah, can you see those cannons sticking out of the windows?' he asked, pointing, 'probably loaded too. You'd think twice about attacking that. It looks impregnable.'

Cannon on the streets of Muscat

Once again they were made welcome by members of the SAF and taken on a guided tour of the city. They were also taken to SAF Headquarters. Chas was naturally interested in the telecommunications equipment and the radio set up the SAF had. He was shown the technical workshop where a familiar face greeted him.

'Chas Pirie, what a great surprise! I didn't know you were with the QDGs.'

'Blossom! And I didn't know you were with the SAF!'

It was Blossom Cartwright, an Army Apprentice colleague; so named because he blushed at the slightest provocation. His real name was Steve.

Chas explained, 'I'm actually with the TOS, but on loan to QDG to provide the link back to Sharjah,'

He shook his head in disbelief. 'Well, blow me down! What a surprise to see you.'

'You guys have picked a good time to visit.' Blossom told him. There'll be a big ceremony tomorrow, when delegations from all the tribes meet up and parley with the Sultan. Fierce warriors all armed to the teeth, it's positively feudal.'

The following day they took up a vantage point from where they could watch the purposeful and determined looking delegation march up the street, on their way to the Sultan's palace to air their grievances and settle their disputes.

Blossom turned to Chas, 'Quite something, eh? Would you like to see the prison?'

Chas hesitated, 'err, it's not a bottle dungeon, is it?'

'No, mate; not like Nizwa. It's OK, you'll see.'

They walked through the wide, paved streets, passed by some huge cannons and came to a large, ornately carved wooden door. A uniformed guard in starched khaki shirt and shorts came out to meet them. The tour was interesting and conditions were altogether more hygienic than those at Nizwa.

After leaving the prison, Blossom turned to Chas,

'Fancy a cup of coffee?'
'Well, yes. There wasn't much in Nizwa. Do you have cafés here?'
'Oh, yes, but this one does have a surprise,' Blossom said, with a mysterious look.

Entrance to the prison in Muscat City

The place was much like any other Arab coffee shop: chairs and tables, some inside and some out. An ancient fan slowly turned, barely moving the air. Groups of Arab men sat smoking cigarettes and sipping the strong, Arab coffee. Thick and black was how they liked it. There was a hubble -bubble pipe in the corner where three elderly, white bearded men were engaged in conversation and passing the mouthpiece around. Blossom found a table and ordered.

In most parts of Arabia, everywhere one goes, flies are a constant annoyance. Inside this particular café there seemed to be none. Chas looked around and saw what appeared to be a moving mass of black on the ceiling. What on earth could it be?

'I see you've spotted the surprise', said Blossom, 'it's nothing but a swarming mass of flies. There's a rotting stingray wing on a hook, up there, and all the flies make straight for it. So there's none down here. The patrons can enjoy their coffee without having to swat flies all the time. Neat isn't it? It's probably been the fly catcher of choice for a thousand years!'

Chas joined the OC and the sergeant again that evening, and the whisky bottle did the rounds once more. Chas was intrigued by the cap badge of the QDG.

'Sir, is that an Austrian eagle? I mean, it has two heads and it's quite an unusual design. I've been trying to think where I've seen it before.'

'You're quite right, Chas. It is an Austrian eagle. Arch Duke Ferdinand himself, the one who got shot in Sarajevo, the event which triggered the start of the First World War, was once the Colonel-in-Chief of the QDG. It was one of those family connections through Queen Victoria. During the last war we weren't allowed to wear the badge. The Austrians had thrown in their lot with the Germans and the War Office were concerned we would be seen to be sporting an emblem of the other side. We couldn't even play our quick march, 'Radetzky'. A real shame, because it's such a damn good march. Written by Johann Strauss the elder, did you know that?'

'No, sir, I know the tune, of course, but I didn't know who wrote it.'

'We're all pals in NATO now, of course, so we've got our cap badge back and the march as well.'

The OC stood up, stretched and yawned. 'We're leaving Muscat tomorrow, corporal, and heading North. Firstly, to rendezvous with a TwinPin that's bringing the mail. After that, we head up the coast for a little R and R. We'll visit Sohar. It'll be our last port of call before heading back to Sharjah.'

Chas recalled the message he received the previous day about the Twin Pioneer aircraft.

These small, twin engine planes, made by Scottish Aviation, could land on the smallest and roughest of airstrips. The RAF operated a regular mail and emergency supplies service throughout the British Arabian area.

Once again, the procession of Ferrets and Land Rovers headed out until they came to what passed for an airstrip. After a while, a faint drone and a tiny speck on the horizon announced the arrival of the Twinpin. It touched down, kicking up a cloud of dust, then turned and taxied towards them.

The RAF pilot emerged, carrying a sack of mail. Letters from home are a key morale booster for troops anywhere. Out on patrol in a strange country, receiving mail raised everyone's spirits. There was even one for Chas. Some kind person had forwarded it to him from Sharjah. It was a letter from his home in Edinburgh. His mother wrote that it was cold, wet and windy in Auld Reekie. What a contrast to here, he thought.

A young local boy rode up on his donkey, curious to see the aeroplane. Chas had an idea. With a bit of persuasion, he managed to create a picture that summed up transport in Muscat. The old and the new: a donkey, a Land Rover and the Twinpin.

That's a picture for my mum and dad, he thought.

That night, they camped among palm trees further up the coast. The fresh sea breeze was very pleasant. They spent a few days relaxing by the sea, swimming and playing volleyball among the palms. After that, the patrol continued north to Sohar, where they witnessed the SAF on parade and changing guard in the compound. They wore the same type of shirt as the TOS, but blue and white, rather than red and white Shemaghs.

Three modes of transport: Donkey, Land Rover and Twin-Pin

A' Squadron Ferrets under the palms in Muscat

Inspecting the SAF guard in

At last, after spending three weeks touring through Muscat and Oman, it was time to say goodbye to their hosts. Chas sat in his Land Rover, gazing out the window, lost in his own thoughts. It had been an amazing experience and one that would stay with him for a long time. He was aware of the OC approaching.

'Have you enjoyed it, then, corporal?' he asked.

'Yes, sir, I certainly have. There can't be many places like this in the world anymore, and I don't suppose it will last much longer. Sooner or later, civilization will invade, and it will change; perhaps not all for the better.'

'Yes, the old Sultan can't hold back the 20th Century forever. I'm glad we got to see it like this.'

12

TOS DHOW TO THE RESCUE!

Hugh Nicklin Royal Signals

The communications centre door burst open and in strode Sergeant Major Ash. This spells trouble, I thought. What have I done now? It was an early morning in November 1966 and I was tired after being on nightshift as communications supervisor. I was just waiting to hand over, ready for a hearty breakfast and then bed.

'Corporal Nicklin, the OC wants to see you in his office just as soon as you come off shift.' This did indeed sound ominous -- what did Major Morris, head of the Signals Squadron, want with me? I knocked on his door.

'Come in'.

I marched in, stood to attention and saluted. 'SSM Ash told me you wanted to see me, sir.'

'Yes, I do. All right, corporal, you can relax. Stand at ease.'

This was beginning to sound a bit better.

'You know there is a very big exercise coming up with LFPG in Bahrain and the TOS'

I nodded. Land Forces Persian Gulf was the HQ of Britain's Middle East presence.

'Well, I have an interesting assignment for you.'

Now I was intrigued and Major Morris had my undivided attention.

'This exercise is going to involve tanks, with LCTs landing them on the Muscat coast. Some Royal Navy ships are involved; putting Royal Marines ashore and a Battalion of the Parachute Regiment will drop on the beach. I want you to take the regimental dhow and be there when they do, just in case any miss the DZ and fall in the sea. You are to act as air/sea rescue.'

This sounded absolutely great. 'Yes, sir, I understand. I've just a couple of questions.'

The major nodded.

'When do I go, sir; how long will I be at sea, and is anyone going with me?'

'You will be on your own, apart from the Arab crew, of course. You've got two days to get prepared and you should be away for about a week. But you'd better make sure you have enough rations for 10 days, just in case. Go and see Staff Sergeant Allcock tomorrow and get kitted out with a C13 radio, batteries and generator. You will also need an OTP cypher pack, plus call signs and frequency allocation. Do you have any other questions?'

'What about my shifts in the Comcen sir?'

'Don't worry about that, corporal, it's all been taken care of. Just go and get some sleep now, and get prepared to be down at the dock in Dubai by 1000hrs in two days time, with all your gear. You'll be sailing on the tide at 1100hrs. All clear with that?'

'Yes, sir, thank you.'

'OK, dismiss' I saluted and marched out.

Editor: note the rapid development taking place along the shores of Dubai Creek during this period

The TOS dhow at Dubai Quay

The following day, I collected my radio and all its associated kit from the signals Quartermaster stores. Staff Sergeant Allcock was his usual, taciturn self.

'Staff, do you have anything for rescuing paras who drop in the sea, like floats or lifesaving rings?'

'What do think this is, the RNLI? It's a signals store, we do radio and assorted communications gear, not bloody lifeboats! Use your initiative, corporal.'

I racked my brains while wandering around the camp.

After an hour of scrounging, all I had to show for it were a few lengths of rope and a bottle of brandy that I bought from the NAAFI shop. My logic was, if brandy is good enough for St. Bernard dogs in the Swiss mountains, then it would probably do to revive a few sodden paratroopers.

In the shadow of the stores, I spread out all the radio kit and tested everything. It was my responsibility to ensure every piece of equipment functioned perfectly before I sailed. I soon had the portable generator chugging away, and after connecting up the transmitter, the receiver, the aerial tuning unit and finally the large lead/acid batteries, the C13 was humming. I tuned it to the TOS network frequency and transmitted a signal strength check with the Morse key. It must have sounded pretty loud in the nearby comcen, the signal probably blasted the ears of the operator. Satisfied that everything worked, I returned it to the stores, ready to be collected in the morning. I would test it all again once I was on board the dhow.

Earlier that morning, I had attended the ops room briefing with a group of TOS officers and senior NCOs. We were told where all the expected landings and troop movements of the exercise were going to take place, and had them pointed out to us on a large wall map. So I was now up to speed with where I needed to be and when. I noted down all the rendezvous details.

At lunchtime I joined Chas Pirie in the cookhouse queue.

'Chas, I need a favour. Are you going down to the beach this afternoon? If you are, could you drop me off in Dubai to do a bit of food shopping?'

'Better than that, Neddy, I'll drop the others off at Sharjah Creek first and give you a hand. Ten days worth of grub is quite a lot.'

We had recently discovered a newly-opened supermarket, managed by an Indian, which, as a marketing ploy, threw in a free carton of 200 cigarettes if you spent even a modest amount. Back in the mid 60's Dubai was developing fast, but was still fairly primitive compared to the huge modern metropolis it would become.

We loaded up with mainly tinned food, eggs, rice, onions, a couple of loaves of bread and, of course, curry powder. There was no refrigeration on board the dhow and although the weather was cooler in November, it would still be a warm 25 - 30 degrees C during the day, so fresh produce would not last. Our smiling Indian friend at the checkout recognized us as frequent shoppers for our trips upcountry and gave us 400 Rothmans, king size. Excellent -- a carton each!

We stowed our shopping in the Land Rover and headed back to pick up the guys from the beach.

I arrived at the dockside in Dubai the following morning, and found where the dhow was berthed. There was a fair quantity of gear to load, so I started taking it aboard.

With big, friendly smiles, members of the crew came to assist me, shaking my hand, welcoming me aboard and making all the usual greetings.

'Salaam Alikum'

'Alikum Salaam. Kefharlak' (Greetings. How are you?)

My C13 HF radio on the deck of the TOS dhow.
Note the packet of Rothmans close to hand.

By 1000h we had everything stowed where I wanted it. The radio was lodged just below the gunwale, midway down the port side. Soon, with the crew's assistance, I had a long wire aerial strung up in the boat's rigging and all my radio modules plugged together and working. The generator coughed into life and chugged away happily. Communications were established with Sharjah and I could now relax.

Promptly at 11am, the TOS dhow slipped its moorings and moved into Dubai Creek. I was excited, elated and very much looking forward to my adventure on the high seas. The deck throbbed beneath my feet, the powerful twin Gardner diesels in the bowels of the boat were gently ticking over as we headed for the open sea. This was no leisurely sailing dhow, it had a turn of speed capable of catching any pirate vessel, gun runner or illegal immigrant craft.

We left the creek and the deck vibration increased as the engines opened up. Turning right, we headed up the coast towards Sharjah, Ajman and Ras al Khaimah. We would eventually pass the northern tip of Muscat and leave the Arabian Gulf. I sat on the deck, my shemagh flapping in the breeze, watching the coast slip by and trying to identify each area on my map as we passed it. The scenery was mainly dry, light brown-yellow desert, interspersed with the occasional collection of low white buildings.

Fishing boats were moored close by. The sun shone without a cloud in the sky and I was enjoying the ride.

The crew had been bustling around, getting the dhow ready, but now that we were cruising, they settled into a routine. While two of them sat casually chatting at the stern, a third held the tiller, with another keeping watch at the bow. The remaining two had gone below. Sounds of cooking pots being rattled reminded me that I was a bit peckish. I had brought a few items of salad to use before I would be obliged to live on dry rations, so I rummaged in my ammo box for the makings of lunch. I enjoyed a cheese salad sandwich while the kettle boiled on my camping gaz stove. I sat on the deck, contentedly sipping hot, sweet tea and smoking a cigarette in the warm afternoon sunshine. I did indeed feel that I was on a cruise.

To relieve the boredom, I had packed a few books so that I could catch up on my reading, but surprisingly, I couldn't concentrate, preferring instead just to sit and watch the world go by. We had three days sailing before the first rendezvous. Fortunately, the crew, who knew this coastline like the back of their hands, had been fully briefed by a fluent Arabic speaker, which was just as well as they spoke almost no English. My grasp of Arabic was rudimentary, but adequate for the essentials of who, what, where and when. Any longer conversation and I was struggling. The TOS officers underwent a three months' intensive Arabic course in Aden before arriving in Sharjah. Us junior ranks had to pick up what we could on the job.

Mealtime aboard the Dhow

The crew did like to confirm the details of the plan with me several times a day. I think they derived quite a bit of amusement at my expense as I valiantly attempted to explain things in my halting, disjointed phrases and mispronounced words.

As the afternoon sped by, my thoughts turned to preparations for my evening meal and sleeping arrangements.

In mid summer, day and night were split evenly into two, twelve - hour chunks as we were so close to the tropic of Cancer. In wintertime, daylight was an hour shorter. There is no long summer twilight as in northern latitudes. It gets dark very quickly once that ball of flame dips beneath the horizon. My camp bed was speedily assembled and a sleeping bag placed on top of it. I figured the camp bed would reduce the deck vibration and allow for a better nights sleep. At dusk, it was time for my call to Sharjah. The C13 was humming as I banged out a quick message on the Morse key to say progress was as expected and there was nothing to report. Sharjah acknowledged and said there were no messages for me. With that I signed off and shut down.

Squatting on the deck, I peeled a couple of onions and chopped them up. My frying pan was on one ring of the gaz cooker and a pan of rice on the other. To thrive in the TOS, one needed to be an accomplished cook, with a handful of recipes that always worked. One could survive by simply warming up a tin of something, or other. But where was the fun in that? We were frequently up country and on our own, without recourse to a cookhouse; that was part of the appeal of life in the TOS, camping out in the desert and knocking up something tasty. Recipes and culinary tips were exchanged over pints of beer in the Scouts Club, with much heated discussion about the best way to fry onions and exactly when to introduce the curry powder and tomato puree. I was glad I had been a boy scout and learned how to cook al fresco, using whatever was to hand. My gastronomic delight for the first evening aboard the dhow was tuna and sweet corn curry, with rice, accompanied by mango chutney and a mug of tea. This was followed by tinned pineapples and cream.

I sat by my radio with the meal perched on my knee. The strong smell of my Indian curry, mingling with the crew's milder and more aromatic fish curry with cardamoms and mint, wafted through the night air.

While one member of the crew held the tiller, the remainder sat around a large, brass platter, placed on the deck and piled high with rice and big chunks of freshly curried fish. They ate with their right hands, while chatting and laughing, their faces animated in the light of a hurricane lamp hung on the mast. We smiled at each other.

'Mungarheear tamaam?' (Is your food good?) I asked.

'Enam, mara whahid tamaam, al hum dil Allah' (Yes, excellent, thanks be to Allah), one of them replied, and we all laughed together.

By 1930, finding myself to be surprisingly tired, I climbed into bed.

The dhow was now at anchor, with the engines switched off, a short distance from the coast at their chosen overnight location. The crew sat at the stern, chatting and passing a hubble-bubble pipe between them. The distinctive bubbling sound drifted to me on the quiet night air, along with the sweet smell of spangles mixed with tobacco smoke.

It was the custom to add flavoursome crystals to the tobacco to make it more interesting. I found it quite soporific and, together with the gentle rocking of the swell, I was soon fast asleep, zipped up in my sleeping bag to help keep the cold out.

A little after first light, I was awake enough to witness the crew at prayer; kneeling down and facing Mecca with foreheads touching the deck. I boiled a kettle and washed and shaved as best I could. Then I visited the heads, a rudimentary arrangement near the stern, where one simply perched over the side on a rickety wooden framework. A luxury cruise with en suite staterooms this was not.

I fancied fried eggs on toast for breakfast. Frying eggs is not a problem on a camping gaz cooker, but making toast is quite another matter. One either prods a slice of bread with a fork and holds it over the flame, usually resulting in burnt fingers, or the bread is tossed into the pan and singed on each side. Neither arrangement is entirely satisfactory, but when you are hungry it still tastes pretty good.

After I had made my morning radio contact with Sharjah, we weighed anchor and set off once more, cruising up the coastline, which was becoming more mountainous with occasional patches of green vegetation. One of the crew, casually line fishing off the side, caught three small fish and another larger one.

We were not alone on the sea, two grey Royal Navy ships passed, some distance away; too far off for me to be able to read their names. A much larger ship, the RCT Arezzo, sailed closer. I waved. A few of the soldiers on deck waved back. I remembered that Arezzo (an army ship) was loaded with troops and tanks which would be landed on the beach as support for the paras, once they had secured the area.

By evening, we had sailed past the tip of the Muscat peninsular and turned right, leaving the Arabian Gulf, entering the Indian Ocean and heading for the Gulf of Oman. Once again, we anchored for the night, some way off from where huge cliffs towered.

The evening meal was a repeat of the previous day's ritual, but I made myself some spaghetti bolognaise, while the crew cooked their catch of the day with different spices.

The hubble-bubble was soon fired up. As they sat around chatting and puffing at it in turns, I made my contact with Sharjah and turned in for the night.

The next morning we headed south towards our rendezvous where we would drop anchor for the night and await the following day's early morning parachute drop. In addition to my radio contact schedule with Sharjah, I now had to break into the TOS tactical Squadron's voice network as 'A' Squadron was deployed inland, near Khawr Fakkan, and I needed to announce my arrival. I changed frequency on the C13, turned the coffee grinder handle on the ATU for maximum power on the dial, pushed the microphone to my face and hit the pressel.

'Hello 88. This is 47, radio check, over.'

These were the first words I had uttered in English for three days. It felt most odd.

'Hello 47, this is 88, receiving you loud and clear. Are you in position?'

I recognized the voice of Captain Curtis of 'A' Squadron. '47, roger. Affirmative, we are in position and standing by.'

'88 roger, out.'

After another excellent night's sleep aboard the dhow (I was really getting into this sailing lark) I awoke with the dawn. This was the big day.

After breakfast of eggs, tinned sausages, beans and a big mug of tea, I checked my air/sea rescue kit – rope and brandy. It really wasn't much, but I hoped the crew would lend me a hand to fish anyone out of the water. The previous evening I had performed a charade for the crew; imitating paratroopers jumping out of a plane and falling in the sea. Imitating how we would cruise by, pluck them from Poseidon's watery grasp and hoist them aboard. With much laughter and wry amusement at my antics, they understood what we had to do, but I had to do a repeat performance because they pretended not to understand what I was getting at the first time. Clearly they enjoyed watching me make a complete prat of myself.

With the engines on low revs, we patrolled some two hundred metres from the beach DZ, going back and forth. Meanwhile, I was scanning the western sky for the first sight of the fat-bellied Beverley aircraft. Shortly after 0900, I spotted them a little to the north west of us.

'Here they come,' I yelled in English and pointed skywards.

There were three of them, flying in line ahead, as they turned right to bring themselves parallel to the coast. I could see that the doors were open as the first of them descended to 1,000 feet and lined up the intended DZ, a long sandy beach, in its sights. My memories of jumping out of a Beverley were vivid and I knew exactly what it would be like to be in the leading stick. The tense faces beneath the helmets, the huge containers of kit strapped to their fronts as they executed the Abingdon two step down the plane.

'Stand up. Hook up. Red light on. Stand in the door.'
Shuffle, shuffle, shuffle. A pause, and then, 'Green light on. Go, Go, Go….'

The jump from a Beverley B

Dozens of small, black shapes were spilling out from both side doors and from the trap door in the Beverley's tail. Dozens of khaki chutes inflated like brown mushrooms in the sky. Containers were released on tethers and swung below each man. Within less than a minute, the first paras had landed on the beach. None of them fell in to the sea. I felt a mixture of disappointment and relief. Damn! There's no-one for us to rescue. On second thoughts, thank God there isn't! I consoled myself with the thought that the next two planes might fare less well and miss the DZ. They didn't.

The RAF were clearly having a good day. It had been a faultless mission. Sometimes, a follow-up drop of heavy equipment and vehicles is made with multiple chutes attached to each platform of kit, but not today. The tanks and other support troops were being landed by *Arezzo*. The other landing craft would provide the necessary transport and equipment.

The beach was now a swarming mass of bodies, releasing their chutes and opening containers to remove weapons before they assembled in groups ready to move inland. There didn't appear to be any casualties; everyone was up and moving. On a para drop of this size, there are usually a few injuries, such as twisted or broken ankles, but not today.

The beach was soon deserted, with the last of the paras just visible in the distance, marching away.

After my initial call to Sharjah, I switched to the local tactical network and had the radio on standby all morning. Once the drop was completed, I reported that the operation had been a success and there had been no need for our rescue services. We were told to standby and hold station for the present. So we lowered the anchor and turned off the engines awaiting further orders. It was still only just after 1000hrs The whole deployment episode had taken less than an hour and they had already disappeared from our sight. The tank landings were taking place on another beach. They were due to rendezvous with the paras somewhere inland. Our job was done -- even though it had really never started!

We stayed there all day and night. The following morning on the tactical network again, I was told to contact Sharjah, as there were urgent messages for me. This was strange, I had already completed my Sharjah contact a couple of hours earlier and there had been no traffic for me at that time

Changing frequency on the C13 once again, I soon regained contact with Sharjah comcen. A high priority, operational immediate, message in code was waiting for me. I took it down as best I could as I sat on the deck, hoping my pencil wouldn't break as I noted each five letter sequence of the encoded message. As soon as I'd receipted it, I set to work with my one time pad (OTP) codebook and unscrambled it.

'You are to rendezvous with RCT *Arezzo* at grid reference XX,YY, as soon as possible. *Arezzo*'s radio is out of action and you are to act as relay. Further messages will be sent to you to pass to the officer in charge. You must remain with the ship until further notice. Acknowledge receipt and confirm understanding.'

Wow, I thought, this really is exciting! Hastily, I encoded an acknowledgement, confirmed that I understood what I needed to do, and sent it back to Sharjah. Then I informed the crew about what was required of us, and why. With the map spread out on the deck, I marked the RV point and after a lengthy discussion, during which I repeated what the problem with Arezzo was (again more play acting and pointing at my radio) The crew were finally satisfied with my explanation, so we weighed anchor and sped northwards.

During the journey, I was kept busy taking down messages for *Arezzo*. There were five of them. Two were lengthy, running to several pages, and all of them were in cypher. Fortunately, they were not for me, and anyway my OTP cypher kit could not unscramble them.

It was late afternoon by the time we spotted *Arezzo* and drew up alongside. It was cooler now, so I had donned my warm, camouflaged para smock over my TOS grey shirt. Wearing my shemagh and clutching a bunch of messages, I scrambled aboard the rocking and rolling army vessel where an officer was waiting for me. I stood to attention and saluted.

Smoking a Hubble-Bubble while admiring the view.

During the journey, I was kept busy taking down messages for *Arezzo*. There were five of them. Two were lengthy, running to several pages, and all of them were in cypher. Fortunately, they were not for me, and anyway my OTP cypher kit could not unscramble them.

It was late afternoon by the time we spotted *Arezzo* and drew up alongside. It was cooler now, so I had donned my warm, camouflaged para smock over my TOS grey shirt. Wearing my shemagh and clutching a bunch of messages, I scrambled aboard the rocking and rolling army vessel where an officer was waiting for me. I stood to attention and saluted.

'Lance Corporal Nicklin, Trucial Oman Scouts, sir. I understand your radio is out of action. I have these messages for you from Bahrain.'

'Oh, you are English. You look so brown I thought you were an Arab.'

After four days spent sitting directly beneath the Arabian sun, it was no small wonder. I felt burnt to a crisp.

He took the messages and told me to wait aboard while they were decoded and a reply was prepared.

'Let me introduce you to our chief Signaller. He will look after you. Follow me, corporal.'

RCT Arezzo passing close by

I was led to the radio room, where a familiar face awaited me.
'Harry Walkden!' I exclaimed. 'What the hell are you doing here?'
'Hello, Neddy, it's good to see you, mate.'
'Oh, that's good. You know one another,' the captain said, with a smile. 'I will leave you in Corporal Walkden's capable hands.'
'We worked together in Germany, sir.'
After the captain had left, Harry winked and asked, 'Fancy a beer, mate?'
'Oh, yes please, that sounds just the ticket, Harry.' I had deliberately not taken any beer with me for two reasons. One, it is difficult to keep cold, and two, out of respect for my Arab Muslim crew who may not appreciate the blatant guzzling of alcohol in their presence.

Harry led me to the mess room and a huge fridge which appeared to contain nothing but beer. After my period of abstinence it was an Aladdin's cave of beery delight.
Supping chilled Carlsberg with Harry was an unexpected pleasure, as we caught up on what had happened to us during the couple of years since we had shared a D11 radio truck on a two week assignment with the Royal Engineers in Hamelin. I seem to remember the majority of the time was spent in the bar and very little on the radio.
'So what's up with the ship's radio?' I asked.

'Power supply. A key component has gone kaput, so we can't get either the receiver or the transmitter working. Sod's law makes it a part that we don't carry a spare for. Apparently, it never goes wrong. The radio itself is a naval Marconi set, quite closely related to the D11s we had in Lippstadt. You would probably find your way round it quite quickly.'

'What about backup radios? You must have other kit.'

'Yes, we do, but they are mainly VHF short range, ship to shore stuff. Not long range HF. What kit have you got on that dhow thing?'

'C13. It works well enough. Solid, reliable and built like a tank. I have it sat on the deck with an aerial running up the mast and into the rigging.' Harry smiled and nodded.

I smiled back, shaking my head in disbelief. 'You know, Harry, this is really weird. I haven't spoken English to anyone for nearly a week, other than three words on the radio, and all of a sudden, I get to enjoy a beer and sit and chat with an old mate, in the middle of the Indian Ocean. You simply couldn't make it up!'

Drawing alongside Arezzo and preparing to board

The cypher decrypt was taking its time, so we had another beer and carried on chatting and laughing. We were sipping the dregs of the second can when the captain walked in.

'Here you are, corporal, there are three messages. The top one is to be transmitted first as it's the most urgent. You will need to hang around until morning when we expect a spare part for the radio to arrive.'

'Yes, sir, I was instructed to stay here until further notice. We will anchor a short way out and report back here in the morning, with any further traffic I receive from Bahrain.'

I saluted and turned to go. 'Good night, Harry. I hope to see you in the morning'

Back on board, the crew were all ears about what was to happen next. I told them we had to hold station close to *Arezzo* until released.

It was well after dark when I turned on the C13 and started transmitting my messages to Sharjah for forwarding to LFPG at Jufair, Bahrain. It took a while to send. The two cans of beer had done nothing to improve my skill with a Morse key, but eventually the messages were acknowledged and I started to think about what I could rustle up for supper. I was starving. I left the radio on, listening out, just in case Sharjah wanted me to re-transmit a portion of the messages because their cypher machine was unable to unscramble it.

There was to be no exotic curry tonight, just a can of mushroom soup, some biscuits and a tin of mixed fruit.

At 2200h, with no further traffic for me, I shut the receiver down and climbed into bed.

Soon after sunrise and a reviving cup of tea, I turned the C13 on again and enquired whether there was anything for me. Two messages, in cypher again. I sat scribbling for all I was worth, turning page after page on my message pad. At about 0800h, we came alongside *Arezzo* again and I scrambled up the ladder to her deck, to be greeted by the captain

'I have another two messages for you, sir.' I told him.

'Thank you, corporal. Would you care to have some breakfast with us while you wait for a reply?'

'Thank you, sir, that's most kind of you.'

My old friend, Harry, ushered me into the dining area and we recommenced our chat of the night before over a hot plate of freshly scrambled eggs, bacon, tomatoes, mushrooms and real toast and marmalade; accompanied by genuine, aromatic coffee, not instant. It was heaven.

I stayed on board *Arezzo* until 1000hrs, very much enjoying their hospitality as I waited. The captain reappeared eventually, holding out another clutch of signals to be sent. 'Thank you, corporal, we do appreciate your timely appearance in our hour of need. The good news is, we expect a spare part to arrive later this morning. Once that is installed and working, you can be on your way.'

'Thank you, sir. I'm delighted to be able to help out, and thank you for the excellent breakfast sir; it was most enjoyable.'

Back on board the dhow, I informed the crew that we were likely to be free to return home by midday, if all went well.

Hammering out long messages on the Morse key was causing me to develop a sore wrist! Too much traffic! The C13's key was a robust, but clumpy affair, designed to be operated in tanks for short messages sent at the relatively low speed of ten or twelve words a minute. The comcen keys were rather more delicate and highly tuned; in the hands of a skilled operator, speeds in excess of thirty words a minute were possible.

Eventually, the messages were sent and acknowledged. As I completed the last of them, a shout went up from the crew. A Royal Navy frigate had been sighted heading for *Arezzo*. She drew near and dropped off a small boat which sped towards the army vessel and tied up alongside. A sailor, clutching a parcel, hopped out and scrambled up the ladder. The much needed spare part for the radio was being delivered. About thirty minutes later, I noticed an Aldis lamp flashing at us from *Arezzo*'s bridge, so I instructed the crew to bring us alongside. The captain held a megaphone.

'Radio all working now. You may depart. And thank you, TOS dhow.'

We all waved acknowledgment and I saluted. It felt like the right thing to do as the crew gunned the engines and we headed for home.

I sensed the crew was anxious to get home to their families now that we were released from further duty.

As we cut through the water at high speed, they said they would drive on through the night, and we would arrive in Dubai early next morning. I left it up to them. It was their boat and their competence and seamanship was something I was not in a position to question. The deck was vibrating harder than at any time in our voyage. The crew certainly had the hammer down. Cooking up what was left in my ammo box of goodies, I savoured my last night aboard with a monster beef curry, vegetables and chicken.

The crew did not indulge in their usual leisurely platter while sitting around for hours, talking and smoking. Instead, they had some khobz bread with cold meat and tea, as they busied themselves, either down in the engine room, or adjusting things on deck and generally tidying stuff away.

Waving farewell to Arezzo

I made my last call to Sharjah, stating that we were homeward bound and requesting a pick up from the docks in the morning.

Just for once there were no messages for me. I snuggled down in my sleeping bag, trying to ignore the vibrating deck. The job was done. We had performed well; turned up at locations on time, accomplished our tasks and even helped out a vessel in distress.

I awoke to total pandemonium, it was 0200hrs. The crew were shouting in alarm as the dhow suddenly lurched to starboard. Looking ahead, I saw a massive wall of wooden planks rushing towards me. Crash! The impact threw me out of my camp bed and sent me rolling across the deck, still in my sleeping bag. I struggled to unzip it and get out, but it had stuck fast. This is it, I thought. We are going to sink and I'm going to drown because I can't get out of this bloody sleeping bag! This is my nightmare coming true!

We scraped down the side of the unknown vessel with a sickening, tortured sound of splintering wood.

With a last desperate tug, the zip gave way and I scrambled out of the sleeping bag. Being on the port side I had been closest to the impact. We had struck an unlit boat, moored further out than usual. For safety reasons, boats that were moored near the shore had a light high on the mast, which remained lit all night long. But not this one! The thought running through my head was that we were definitely going to sink. How far was it to the shore? Could I swim to it? Sod the radio, but what should I do with my cypher pads? Should I try to eat them before jumping overboard?

Fortunately, things soon quietened down. Some of the crew went below while another looked for damage over the forward port side. We were not shipping water and the damage looked mainly superficial. These dhows were made of strong stuff.

After this bit of excitement it was impossible to go back to sleep. I did what all Englishmen do in a crisis. I made a cup of tea. Deciding that, under the circumstances, this was an inadequate response, I opened my bottle of RNLI brandy and took a swig. Sod the Paras and the bloody St. Bernards. I really needed this. Ah, that's a lot better, I thought. So I poured a generous libation into my tea.

The rest of the night passed, as all nights do, and I was glad to see Dubai creek coming up in the early morning light.

We moored in our usual location. Soon, with the crew's assistance, all my gear was stacked on the dockside awaiting my transport. I shook hands with each member of the crew and thanked them for their efforts. We laughed about the night's drama, thankful that we were safely back on dry land. I decided not to mention the incident in my report as the crew weren't that concerned about it.

Back in Sharjah, I handed in all my radio equipment. After reporting to Major Morris and describing the week's activities, he made a few notes and told me to take the rest of the day off. After lunch and a catching-up with some of my signals mates, I wandered over to the Scouts Club for what I thought was a well-earned beer or two. Everyone commented on my tan, which was not surprising, eight days of toasting under the sun while being at sea had rendered me mahogany.

13

THE EMPTY QUARTER

Ron Wildman as told to Hugh Nicklin

Ron Wildman's Liwa Patrol

In January 1967 Cpl Ron Wildman, radio technician of the Trucial Oman Scouts Signals Squadron set off from Sharjah in a Land Rover with an Arab driver heading West to Mirfa. It was a bitterly cold eight hour journey over the inland route as the easier coastal route was unusable because the sabkha was treacherous after recent rain. He had plenty of time to contemplate what lay ahead of him on a patrol into the most inhospitable region of Arabia we called the Liwa, but known by a far more sinister name, The Empty Quarter -- a desert the size of France and Spain combined. At last the welcome sight of a line of Dodge Power Wagons (DPW) greeted him as they pulled into Mirfa camp, our most Westerly and desolate outpost.

It comprised of a row of tents on the beach below a scarp with the kakhi-coloured desert stretching in every direction except north where the shallow blue coastal waters and sandbars of the Arabian Gulf reached out to the horizon. The DPWs looked capable and businesslike with their massive balloon tyres and long bonnets concealing huge 4.1 litre engines. If anything could carve a path through the Empty Quarter's sea of sand it would be these monsters. As Ron opened the door to get out, the officer commanding (OC) Mirfa squadron ran across a sand dune towards him.

'A' Squadron DPWs lined up

'Come on, corporal, I want you to take an un-posed photo in the desert for my mum.'

An expensive Nikon was immediately thrust into Ron's hands. As greetings went this was an unusual one – usually a bit of saluting and standing to attention were involved. However, Ron duly took the 'Me photograph' as we called them, while the officer struck an heroic, but casual stance against the dunes. Then, pulling out his own Minolta, Ron asked the OC to do the same for him. As Ron said afterwards,

'Not quite Dr Livingstone, I presume, but certainly an introduction to remember.'

'Good to have you aboard corporal, we need reliable communications in the Liwa. Do you have a good supply of spare parts and tools to fix the radios?'

'Yes, sir, I do, but you know, sir, these sets, the C11 and C13, are pretty reliable and I really don't expect to have too much to do. Is there anything else I could help with?'

'Well corporal,' he said, after a moments hesitation, 'I do believe there is. We do have a local Bedu guide of course, who I'm assured is very good, but I would also like you to plot our position each day to be certain. You can use a map and compass I presume?'

'Yes, sir, I can.'

'Excellent! You will be taking bearings against three oil fires that are clearly visible for miles. There's a lot of exploration drilling going on round here, which is why this region is strategically important.

And we can't let the Saudis encroach on the Trucial States can we?'

'No, sir, we can't.'

'Oh, and another thing corporal, you will be riding in the fuel wagon which means strictly no smoking, I'm afraid. Would you also be responsible for checking our fuel and water supplies each day? This is crucial as there are almost no wells where we are going and no people. Breaking down and running out of either fuel or water could be fatal.'

'Yes, sir, you can leave that to me. I'll check the levels each day.'

The no-smoking rule was not welcome news as Ron was a twenty-a-day Rothmans man, but he was happy to have something useful to do as he knew the days would be long and probably not much going wrong with the radios to relieve the boredom. The purpose of the Liwa patrol was to look for signs of activity which might suggest incursions across the borders of Trucial Oman. In the past, some of the line of oil drums filled with concrete that marked the border had mysteriously moved. Pitched battles had been fought over territorial rights in the 1950s, in particular, around the, relatively lush, Buraimi Oasis.

This patrol was looking for evidence of vehicle tracks and winter was the best time to do so. The sand was firmer and not so prone to the obliterating desert winds. The operation was to be conducted in secret. All radio communication back to base in Sharjah would be in Morse code and the messages encrypted using a one time pad (OTP), which in its day was one of the most secure technologies available.

The five DPWs set off line astern on a cold, clear early January morning soon after dawn, the huge tyres making easy work across the plain of hard rock covered in sand. A wall of dust streamed behind them in a huge cloud.

After a day of driving along desert tracks they stopped for the night. The Captain walked across to Ron's vehicle.

'Corporal, we are staying the night here. Tomorrow, we'll pick up our guide and go into the Liwa proper. Have you got enough rations and cooking gear?'

'Yes Sir, I brought enough for at least ten days. I'm well prepared, sir, and quite self sufficient. I regularly travel round all the outposts repairing radios.'

'Excellent, we're all going to fend for ourselves this evening and have a proper cookhouse style meal tomorrow.'

Ron soon had his primus stove roaring away and a tasty meal of spaghetti bolognaise prepared.

The following morning they set off once again soon after dawn. After an hour of driving they pulled up at an old barusti hut next to a well. A tall bearded Arab stepped out to greet them carrying the biggest elephant gun Ron had ever seen. He was dressed in brown flowing robes, a brown jacket and a white headdress which had a length of coloured silk scarf skillfully threaded into it. He looked every inch a Bedouin noble standing there holding his camel stick. He also wore a bandolier of huge bullets diagonally across his chest; and in his belt an enormous silver khanjar. He was an impressive gentleman and not someone to argue with.

'Salam Ali Khum'

'Ali khum Salam'

Their guide, a tall, aristocratic looking, bearded Arab

The customary greetings having been exchanged, Mohammed, our aristocratic-looking guide, climbed into the passenger seat of the leading DPW and they were off, heading into the least populated area of the Arabian peninsular, The Empty Quarter.

Ron was awestruck by the seemingly endless dunes, it felt like being on a wild yellow sea of massive waves caught in freeze-frame where the only moving things were the vehicles. But progress was slow. Even with its huge tyres the DPW struggled in the soft sand. They revved hard to climb up the wave of sand and coasted down the other side hoping to get enough momentum to climb some way up the next one. Occasionally they even had to let some air out of the tyres to get a better grip on very soft sand. After six hours they stopped for the night and looked at the mileometer reading – a mere eleven miles progress in the Liwa.
 The plan was to be out for ten days, with what they hoped was a generous quantity of fuel and water in reserve.
 The sun was now low in the sky and it would be dark soon, and very quickly once it dropped below the horizon. There's no twilight in the tropics.
 They made camp in a suitable dip in the dunes. While the hurricane lamps and primus cookers were being fired up for the evening meal, Ron took his prismatic compass and scanned the horizon.
 Sure enough, as darkness fell, an orange glow was visible to the North East, then another to a few degrees East of it and then a third. All three were within a 45-degree arc. It was quite dark now as Ron took bearings at the centre point of each light source jotting the readings on a notepad illuminated by torchlight. Spreading the map out on the sand he aligned the map to North and plotted his bearings to achieve a triangulation. Where the lines crossed was where they were.

And it was indeed about ten or eleven miles from where they had entered the Liwa. So they knew their location and Ron scribbled down the OS grid reference.

After handing it to the OC, Ron was free to enjoy a welcome cigarette as the aroma of chicken curry wafted through the cool night air. It smelt good, and, boy was he hungry after a day of the slowest and most difficult driving he had ever known. Meanwhile Ali Obeyd the signaller had set up his aerial, warmed up the C13 HF radio and tuned it to the frequency of the TOS network ready to transmit back to base. The sound of static and high-pitched Morse code filled the night. After contacting Sharjah and exchanging signal strengths, Ali continued to tap away on his Morse key warning Sharjah to standby for a message.

Sending the SITREP in Morse code. Ali Obeyd

. The SITREP (Situation Report) was short, giving only details of the location and progress. It was coded into cipher groups of five letters each, just so much gobbledegook to anyone listening in. Ali tapped out the message quickly and Sharjah acknowledged receipt, so now the radio could be shut down for the night

Time to eat and everyone was ready for that chicken curry. Sitting on the sand under the stars with Ali getting stuck into his overflowing mess tin of rice and curry (the cook's helpings had been generous), Ron felt content and was sure he would sleep well.

'Did the C13 work OK Ali?'

Ali Obeyd smiled. 'All OK, boss -- Koulish tamaam, inshallah. Alhumdil Allah.'

'Tamaam. Although I really mean, oh bugger, nothing for me to do – I'm off to bed now, see you bukrah.'

Ali laughed out loud. 'Maybe radio be broken tomorrow corporal Ron! Salamit Malam.'

Ron was still chuckling as he climbed into his sleeping bag laid out on the soft sand, he was glad it was a thick one as the temperature was plummeting.

It was cold as the first fingers of light touched the dunes. Ron opened his eyes, revealing signs of activity as the campsite was coming to life. Sounds of soldiers yawning, chatting and laughing as Ron crawled out and got dressed quickly. He pulled on a warm civvy coat, pleased that he'd had the forethought to pack. The cookers were roaring full blast so there would soon be hot tea and breakfast.

In The Empty Quarter

We faced another day of slow progress over the seemingly never ending, shifting ocean of sand. No landmarks at all, just the sun tracing a leisurely arc across the clear azure sky as the day wore on. Again the progress was agonizingly slow, with frequent stops as the great mechanical beasts laboured up hill and down dale. Some stops were for prayers as the Arab soldiers knelt towards Mecca several times a day.

The novelty of the scenery was also beginning to lose its appeal as they drove on a compass bearing with occasional correction from the Arab guide who uncannily seemed to know exactly where he was despite the featureless terrain.

'How far to the well, Mohammed?' asked the OC.

'Seven hours, sahib,' replied the guide.

Distance was not measured in miles, but in hours travelling. And he was right every time. The OC walked over to Ron during one of the many stops.

'How are you getting on?' he asked.

'Fine, Sir. It's a bit slow going though, isn't it?'

'Unfortunately you're right. We're making bloody slow progress. But this would be much more difficult in a Land Rover or Bedford as they just don't have the raw power and massive tyres to get through this stuff.

The guide tells me we're only a mile or so from the border here, not that you can tell because it all looks the same. No one's been out here putting up a barbed wire fence or oil barrels full of concrete to mark it out. We have to trust his knowledge and your compass bearings each day to make sure we stay this side of the border.'

Top of dune looking down on DPWs. An almost vertical drop of several

'Are we following the border on this patrol sir?'
'Yes, we'll keep heading east along it, keeping an eye out for tracks or anything suspicious.'

The days sped by but the miles did not. On a good day twenty miles were covered but most were between ten and fifteen. All the time they searched for tracks. On the third day a lookout shouted excitedly. He had spotted some distinct tracks of a vehicle and raised the alarm. The convoy followed these for a couple of miles but then they petered out completely. Each day Ron checked the bearings at the night stop and the SITREP was sent to base. In the morning, he monitored the fuel and water reserves. So far, so good, but he calculated they were burning fuel at a faster rate than predicted, a concern he raised with the OC that evening when the OC wandered over as Ron was cooking.

'Umm, that smells good, corporal.' The OC had started coming over most evenings when Ron was cooking and cadging a meal. Obviously the Arab fare he was given was not quite the same as Ron's culinary efforts. The officers in these desert outposts did have a lonely life. There was plenty of social life in the Officers' Mess in Sharjah and Manama but hardly any in desolate places like Mirfa. Ron was a capable and accomplished desert cook, as were most members of the signals squadron. We were so frequently up country for both business and pleasure that we got a lot of practice.

'There's plenty here sir, if you'd like some.'

After the meal they sat back and Ron lit a cigarette. 'You know, sir, I'm a bit worried by the rate we're burning fuel. These DPWs are thirsty beasts, and hacking through the sand dunes is really taking it out of them. I don't think we have enough for ten days' patrol sir.'

'Umm, I did wonder about that corporal. We'll have to keep a close watch on consumption. Don't want to run out here in the middle of nowhere, do we?'

'No sir, it could be disastrous.'

'Well, once again, thank you for another of your delicious meals. Time to get some sleep, I think. Good night, corporal.'

'Good night, sir.'

When he'd gone, Ron thought, at least he could have offered to do the washing up.

Following the border they came across the occasional well, but they were very few and far between. The Arab guide had such a feel for the area he was always able to lead the convoy directly to them. Every opportunity to fill up with water was taken.

On the fourth day the dunes appeared to be getting ever bigger as the DPWs huffed and puffed upwards to the top of a knife edge ridge. The lead DPW suddenly tipped forward and stopped. One side had been a gentle climb, but the other was concave where the wind had worn it away and was almost a vertical descent. With its four-wheel drive and low ratio gears screaming, it made no forward progress, throwing up great clouds of sand as it dug itself in.

'Stop,' yelled the OC, 'turn the bloody engine off'.

An assessment was conducted and several attempts were made to free the stricken vehicle but to no avail.

'It's not working,' said the OC. 'We're going to have to go around and pull it out from below.' The OC, the guide and Ron looked at the map spread out on a DPW bonnet.

'The map's not great for detail because the sand is constantly shifting. But it looks as though our only route is to circle right round here, back the way we've come. Then we can access the bottom of this huge dune. It'll be easier pulling it downward than trying to pull upwards as we are at the moment. Gravity and a lack of grip are working against us.'

Our guide nodded and explained in Arabic what the terrain was like below and the best approach. The OC sighed, 'Either way, it's a long detour. But it looks like our only course of action, because that truck,' he pointed to the stuck DPW, 'despite our best efforts, is going absolutely nowhere.'

So the decision was made to make an excursion round to the other side of the dune and pull it off with winches. However this was not just a couple of miles out of the way. It resulted in a detour of twenty miles and took a day and a half before they were looking up the dune at the stationary DPW again.

Two men slowly climbed the dune with ropes and steel hawsers fed from the front winches of three DPW's. Then they were driven up the slope, line abreast, as far as they would go. Hopefully there would be sufficient rope and cable to reach the stuck vehicle. The men reached the stricken DPW and attached the cables. They turned and gave a thumbs up signal.

'OK, 'said the officer, 'gently does it. Shway, shway. Take up the slack and all three of you, pull,'

Nothing seemed to happen. The DPW remained half buried in the sand. The cable tightened like a bowstring and the winches were straining and the DPW engines were gently revving. Everyone held their breath.

'Steady now, just hang on, gentle pressure,' said the OC.

Suddenly it began to move, slowly at first as the sand, which enveloped it parted and the vehicle emerged. Faster and faster it moved, coming down the hill.

'Keep it straight and keep pulling. We don't want it tumbling over now.'

Finally, the vehicle was at the bottom of the dune, a little dusty, but otherwise none the worse for wear. The driver climbed in, swept sand off the seat, and started the engine. On the third attempt it fired into life. A cheer went up from everyone.

Once the stricken DPW has been successfully dragged out, progress was resumed. On the seventh day more tracks were spotted and once again they were followed heading in the direction of the Saudi border. Everyone was elated as they chased the tracks for a mile across the dunes, but once again they suddenly petered out before reaching the border itself, and no further sign was visible. Disappointed, they pitched camp for the night.

During the preceding week the Arab soldiers had been gathering firewood. Usually this was reasonably plentiful, but here in the Liwa there was precious little. They cooked their flat Khobz bread on the warm embers of a fire. This they had been unable to do all week. A hardship they were not used to. However they now had the back of a DPW loaded up with dried-up gnarled twigs and branches of whatever vegetation could survive in this desolate area. They lit a fire and cooked up their bread once more.

'How's the fuel situation, Corporal?' asked the OC.

'Not so good sir, I think we have enough to head home, but not a lot to spare. But there is enough water for a few days yet'.

'That settles it then, we head back in the morning.'

The following morning Ron looked up at the sky, which had been steadily building up with clouds during the past two days. He was sure he could smell rain in the air. He walked over to the OC.

'Sir, I think it's about to rain,' he smiled knowingly, 'I'm from Manchester, so I know a lot about rain.'

'Well, it does rain here. Not much though, but we sometimes catch the end of the Indian monsoon. Hopefully, we will get back before the sabkha turns to quicksand. Even in a DPW it's not easy going.'

An hour later it was raining lightly as they turned around and headed out of the Liwa. They said goodbye to their guide who had been so accurate and had seen them safely travel through one of the world's last wildernesses.

On the way they saw a huge caravan of camels, which had apparently just come through the Liwa. Ron turned to Ali Obeyed, the signaller,

'Ali, how do they manage to get through the Liwa? We were struggling in powerful DPWs.'
'Ah, corporal sahib, camels can go anywhere and everywhere.'

So they had been eight days in the Liwa and arrived back with very little fuel and a day and half of water, but none of the vehicles broke down and neither did the radios.

Being back on the firmer desert tracks of the plain was a welcome change and once again the DPWs were happily flying along at speed trailing a massive cloud of dust behind them. At the end of our tours with the TOS, we Signallers went our separate ways and lost touch with each other for four decades. Then, forty three years later, thanks to the internet, we managed a reunion in June 2010. Ten old TOS Signallers got together again at the Royal Signals' Association weekend in Blandford. It was just like old times. At the same event each year there is a march past on the parade ground and the band plays. We proudly stride along in our red and white shemaghs, standing out among 600 other old Signallers. We raise the biggest cheer from the audience and everyone wants to know who we are and why we are wearing Arab headdress.

TOS Signalman at a rreunion in Blandford in 2010.

Standing from left: Steve Cartwright, Dave Hobson, Mick Wilson, Roger Baines, Chas Pirie, Don MacSween and Hugh Nicklin. Barry Harban and Ron Wildman are seated.

14

SOMEBODY HAD TO PAY THEM!

Joe Hughes RAPC

In 1965 I was a Royal Army Pay Corps corporal attached to the 1st Battalion, Sherwood Foresters Regiment, stationed at Hyderabad Barracks in Colchester, Essex. I was working in the Pay Office and looking forward to my impending posting to 2 Para, which was due in a few weeks time, when I was summoned to the Paymaster's Office by Captain Potts. He informed me that a Pay Corporal was urgently required by the Trucial Oman Scouts. I had no knowledge of the region then known as the Trucial States, but I quickly made enquiries and discovered enough information about the history of the Trucial Oman Scouts to keep me interested in them. Captain Potts and other members of staff encouraged me to apply for the posting, but my mind was finally made up when I saw what the rate of Overseas Allowance was! So within a few weeks I was on my way. We flew from Brize Norton to Sharjah via Bahrain. I seem to remember being accompanied on the flight by a couple of three ton Trucks and a Tank! The aircraft must have been a Beverley or a Hercules?

Inside a Twin Pioneer Aircraft

Upon arrival at RAF Sharjah, I was collected and driven to the TOS Pay Office where I was introduced to the senior NCO, Staff Sergeant Ron Butterfield, and other members of the pay team. The Paymaster was Major Don Tibbey. He was affectionately known as 'Father Tibbey', because he was a generation older than most of us there. The major was a marvellous character with, like myself, a fondness for an occasional tipple. I have very happy memories of our trips together to pay the troops stationed at Manama, Masafi, Burami, etc. We went by Land Rover and, very occasionally, by the fantastic Twin Pioneer Aircraft. 'Father Tibbey' told me that he didn't like travelling on them because of a previous crash that had cost the life of a fellow officer. Major Tibbey was scheduled to be on that flight, but was taken off at the last minute.

The trips by Land Rover were memorable to say the least. There were no roads, no road signs, and the journeys that we took were long and hot. Incredibly, we would sometimes come across a small barusti shack in the middle of the desert, selling cold drinks!

Pay parades were a strange but enjoyable experience. We had to explain to the men, in our rough and ready Arabic, the breakdown of their pay; their basic wage, plus their entitlement to ration allowance (RA), meat entitlement to ration allowance (MERA) and other entitlements.

Everybody liked 'Father Tibbey' and enjoyed his quirky sense of humour. He was a big friend of Major Ken Wilson, the officer commanding 'X' Squadron at Masafi. I had the good fortune and the pleasure of being invited by Major Wilson to the Masafi Officers' Mess during one of our visits.

The 'road' between Sharjah and Manama

The evening concluded with a sword fight between the two officers. We eventually managed to drag them apart. Luckily, no one was seriously injured!

Major Tibbey was one of the longest-serving members of the Trucial Oman Scouts. He eventually passed away while still serving with the Force. He is buried in Sharjah Cemetery. R.I.P. Along with several other ex-TOS members, I visited his grave during our visit to the UAE in 2012. Staff Sergeant Ron Butterfield was a good leader. His relaxed personality made our working days enjoyable and interesting. He wrote several short stories for 'Parade', a popular girlie magazine of the day. I actually wrote a story for him that got published - but I'd rather not go into that!

The other member of the pay team who I remember with great affection was a civilian Indian gentleman called Mr. Bhatia. He immediately made me feel welcome and guided me through the complicated TOS pay and accounts system, and even invited me for a meal with his lovely family who lived in very basic accommodation in Sharjah. Mr Bhatia was a great man with a beautiful family.

Corporal Pete Devlin joined our team in 1966. We also became good friends and I remember the great times we spent together - particularly in the Scouts Club - the regular meeting place for a few beers for other ranks and their guests. Pete also took over from me as the DJ on Forces Radio Sharjah's TOS requests programme.

It's not often that a member of HM forces is given the privilege of serving with a force like the TOS. One would have to become a mercenary to do it today.

None of us who served with them imagined at the time that we were assisting seven Sheikhdoms, still living very much in the Middle Ages, to become a nation of great wealth and influence in the world. Learning the language was not easy, but most of us grasped enough of it to be understood by local people and Arab soldiers. Some members of the Force went on Arabic courses and became quite fluent.

My initial visits to Sharjah Souk and the friendliness of the local people were, for a raw young 21 year old rookie Irishman, quite memorable. The sight of bearded men walking around with great, curved daggers stuck in their belts and rifles over their shoulders; just 'window shopping' like everyone else, was certainly different to a trip to the shopping centre in Colchester!

Most of my colleagues will remember the trips to Dubai - especially shopping at Jashanmals - where I bought my first long playing record album - Barbara Streisand's 'Funny Girl'. I wanted the Beatles, 'Rubber Soul', but it wasn't in stock.

Jashanmals, originally founded by the late Rao Sahib Jashanmal, grew from humble beginnings into a very large wholesale and retail company in the Middle East. Afternoons spent sunbathing and swimming in RAF Sharjah Camp's salt water pool, was relaxing and great fun. Many of us returned there in the evenings, wrapped in a blanket because the temperature had dropped, to watch a film at the outdoor cinema.

One of the places to visit at week-ends was the old Carlton Hotel in Dubai. In those days, it did not sell alcohol, but we were allowed to take our own drinks. I went there with Bill Thitchener and others, and met up with some of the American oil workers we had entertained at the Scouts Club a couple of weeks earlier. Major Tibbey was there that night, along with some other TOS officers. I was pleased to be able to spend some time with him.

'Window' Shopping in Sharjah Souk

Bill got a bit upset because the Americans failed to offer to buy us a drink. They had already enjoyed a free night in the Scouts' Club. A punch-up ensued, during the course of which I got a little battered, ending up on the floor of the upstairs bar.

I couldn't see where Bill was and after I'd managed to get to my feet, I refused to leave until I knew he was all right. Eventually, I got kicked down the stairs and found Bill waiting at the bottom. He looked at me lugubriously as I struggled to my feet, and asked,
'Where the heck have you been, Joe?'

New Year's Eve prompted big celebrations. A fancy dress party was held on a barge on Dubai creek. Invitations to it were exclusive and restricted to local company management and senior officers of the TOS, RAF and other services. My good mate, Dougie Hands, got to hear about the party from a couple of nurses he knew from his regular deliveries to a local hospital. After he told me about the party we developed a cunning plan! Because it was fancy dress, no one would recognise us if we wore the right costumes. We borrowed a couple of appropriate ones from the lads in the RAF who had held a fancy dress party a little earlier.

The outfits were very good - Dougie's was that of a Chinaman, complete with hat, moustache, etc, and mine was a four-foot high cardboard tube in the form of a Rothman's cigarette, with an equally long, matchstick attached to it.

The Scouts Club

We drove from Sharjah to Dubai in a ration truck and parked a couple of hundred yards away from the barge so that nobody would recognise us as gatecrashers.

The entrance to the barge was down a steep ladder. My Rothman's cigarette costume made walking very difficult and getting into the barge even more so.
Basically, I had to hold on to the rails and hobble down the ladder - to the amusement of others at the party.

It was all great fun, but the problem for me was the fact that, thanks to my silly Rothman's cardboard tube, I couldn't sit down. I waited until most of the party goers were tipsy then took it off. Nobody recognized me. I was able to convince everyone that I was the local Rothman's representative!

As you may judge from all this - we of the TOS played hard, but we also worked hard in an extremely harsh environment. That is why we let off steam whenever we had the chance to do so. Memories of the friends I made and the comradeship of others during my stay in a wonderful country, linger on. The Trucial Oman Scouts Association enables old comrades to continue to meet with one another. It is heart-warming for we veterans who were privileged enough to serve with the Trucial Oman Scouts.
'Mashkoor' (Thank you) to the wonderful people of the Trucial States, now the United Arab Emirates. You will be in my thoughts forever.

Joe Hughes on another barge in Dubai in 2010

15

A WESSEX AND TWO ANDOVERS

Bob Todd Royal Signals

One morning, while I was on a course in Catterick, a soldier entered the barrack room. Very excited, he announced,
 'You ought to see what's outside on the parade ground. It's somebody from the Trucial Oman Scouts, and he is in Arab headdress!'
 I didn't see the person at the time and had no idea that I would be his replacement in the TOS.
 I finally met up with him at the Trucial Oman Scouts 60th Anniversary celebration in London in May 2012.

In 1966, I was in Germany, attached to 2nd Field Regiment, Royal Artillery, a posting with which I was not very happy. After seeing a request for volunteers for the TOS on Daily Routine Orders I spoke with my immediate boss. He was a worldly type who, having joined the army towards the end of World War Two had been up and down the ranks more times than a fireman on a ladder. He misinformed me that the TOS was some kind of commando unit in Bahrain, but told me I should go.
 He added that I'd know every sand dune there by the time I came back -- if I did come back, that was. With that rather disturbing thought in mind, I volunteered and was accepted.

Whilst on embarkation leave I received a letter from the Army that provided me with some background information about the TOS, along with all the do's and don'ts involved whilst serving with them. This information included several instructions. One part I found particularly amusing. I was to cut all Marks and Spencer (St Michael) labels from any civilian clothing I was taking with me. The company was owned by a Jewish family, offending any Arab who might be obliged to handle my clothes in a laundry, etc.

Back at the Royal Signals Transit Squadron, I had to fill out various documents. Those about to be posted were asked to confirm their name, number and the unit they were going to. At that time there were still some unusual postings to be had, east of Suez. When people stated they were going to Hong Kong, Singapore, etc, 'Lucky B******s,' was the opinion expressed by those less fortunate. At last it was my turn. When I stated, 'The Trucial Oman Scouts,' a deathly silence went around the room, everybody turning to stare at me.

For the rest of the time I spent at the transit unit, hardly anybody spoke to me. Even today, I still find that when the TOS is mentioned, a glazed look appears in people's eyes, and I have to spend some time explaining about the unit. Maybe they had seen the article in an American magazine, the title of which appears on this page.

The most memorable part of flying to Bahrain was observing the thick plumes of black smoke rising from oil drilling platforms, as they burnt off the excess gas. I sometimes wonder what the environmentalists would say if this practice was carried out today. Upon arrival at Bahrain, I soon discovered that no one knew anything about me. This was the norm, as I found out when I got to Sharjah.

In early December 1966, I arrived at my destination. It was late in the evening, and, of course, no one was expecting me. The RAF Movements clerk arranged for the TOS duty driver to collect me and take me to their HQ.

Someone was summoned from the Sergeants' Mess to arrange my accommodation and get me settled in.

Once I had been allocated a bed, the sergeant, whose name was Steve Cartwright, told me,

'The next place you ought to see is the Scouts Club. You'll meet some of the other guys in there.'

The next day, I was issued with my TOS uniform and introduced to the Arab team I would be working with. One of them was named Rafiq.

He had a stall in Sharjah's souk, where he specialised in selling silver. When he shook my hand, he took a close look at my fingers. The next day, he presented me with a TOS ring. What a difference to the greeting I'd got in Bahrain, where youths had thrown stones at me when I'd stopped to watch them play a game of football!

I proudly wore that ring for over forty five years. It only had to be repaired once, but now it is so battered, it is past wearing.

Soon after my arrival in Sharjah, I had the obligatory interview with the Signal Squadron OC, whose name was Major Williams. He briefed me fully about the role of the TOS; my involvement being principally that of maintaining and inspecting the generators used by the Signallers. This would include 'tech tours', in other words, periodic visits to the TOS outstations. Major Williams told me that I would be going on one of them in a couple of day's time. Captain Crouch, the Squadron's second in command, informed him that this was not possible as new arrivals were required to spend ten days becoming acclimatized before going 'up country'.

My first tech tour would not happen until January.

Christmas was soon upon us and many a happy hour was spent in the Scouts Club.

On Christmas Day, a number of donkeys found themselves rounded up and competing with one another in a 'Derby', of sorts. It was shambolic - and hilarious to watch! Later in the day, I was asked if I would like to pay a visit to the makeshift bars that the RAF, not satisfied with their one 'official' bar, had set up in their billets.

A grand tour started. At the end of it we decided to call in at the swimming pool. Having staggered our way there, we dived in, fully clothed, much to the amusement of the RAF lads in attendance. We emerged to dry ourselves off by rolling in the sand. Then, of course, we had to clean our clothes, so back we went and dived in again. Well, it made sense at the time! After several repetitions of this, the rather more sedate RAF boys began to disappear.

In January, I embarked on my first tech tour, along with Dave Hobson and Steve Cartwright. It was essential that everyone carried out the standard TOS procedure before beginning any journey into the desert. To book out at the comcen, by sending a radio message, informing those at your destination that you are on your way. The locations we were to visit were the Abu Dhabi Political Agency (PA), now the Embassy, Mirfa, Fort Jahili at Buraimi (now Al Ain), Manama, and Masafi. At Mirfa, I was introduced to the 'loo with a view', and told that when occupying this primitive, outdoor facility, I was not to forget to raise the red flag, and to lower it again when I left.

At first, I had no idea how we were finding our way from place to place, but I began to notice various landmarks that helped us point our vehicle in the right direction, and made mental notes of them to help me avoid getting lost during future journeys.

In the spring of 1967, Dave Hobson and I were obliged to attend a MPC (Military Proficiency Course) in Aden at 15 Signal Regiment. We were told to remember that we would be representing the Trucial Oman Scouts, and as such, would be wearing our TOS uniforms. That was all very well, but when we arrived in Aden, dressed as ordered, the signal regiment's RSM was not very happy about it. Dave and I spent the first day being marched from one department to another as the powers that be tried to convince us that we should wear British army uniforms while we were on the course. We were even taken on a visit to the Quartermaster's Stores, where two neat piles of standard army uniforms were waiting for us on the counter. I thought the RSM and RQMS were going to have a fit when both Dave and I refused to sign for the kit.

Rafiq in the Battery Store, checking the specific gravity of the electrolyes

Eventually, we ended up in front of the adjutant, at which point, after some discussion, Dave asked to be returned to Sharjah. He was marched out of the office – with his marching orders! The RSM must have thought, 'One down, one to go.'

The adjutant was also rather concerned about me carrying out drill while wearing the traditional leather sandals issued to me by the TOS. I informed him that they too were part of our uniform and they would not be a problem as far as I was concerned. He gave up on me after that, leaving a rather subdued RSM to march me to the barrack room I was to occupy. The bunks were three high and I had been allocated a top one, directly beneath a hole in the roof. When the RSM saw me gazing up at this, he said,

'Don't worry, that's the result of a mortar attack from some of your Arab mates. Once they know you're here, they won't bomb us!'

I think the last laugh was with me, because, thanks to the shemagh, I was able to conceal the longest hair and sideburns of anyone on any of the courses!

As far as I was concerned, nobody could utter those immortal words, 'Get your bleedin' 'air cut!

An interesting episode concerning the shemagh happened when we were travelling along the Aden Causeway in an open Land Rover. I was sitting in the back, opposite an escort armed with an SMG. As it was rather windy, I wound my shemagh around my face. The escort told me to take it off, pronto, because there was a vehicle following us with some Arabs shaking their fists at us and blowing their vehicle's horn. They had mistaken me for a captive of the British! Thankfully, I was not 'rescued' by the occupants of the car.

On tech tour; taking on water at the crossroads between Dubai, Abu Dhabi, Buraimi and Mirfa

By one of those pleasant coincidences, an uncle and aunt of mine were also in Aden. My uncle was a sergeant in the RAF. In Sharjah, I had been given very little notice that I was going to Aden, so my aunt and uncle didn't know I was there. My uncle was a very keen dingy sailor, so I knew they would most likely be at the sailing club on a Sunday morning. It was a security rule that everyone had to have a comrade with him when they were 'off camp'. So, together with a companion, I set off for the club. After making a few inquiries among the members, it was confirmed that both my aunt and my uncle would be arriving before the first race started. They nearly fell off their moped when they turned up and saw me sitting on the club's patio.

There is a little twist to the events in Aden. In 1972, I was posted in Germany. During the yearly Admin Inspection that took place while I was there, we were visited by a brigadier. My OC at the time tended to get flustered very easily during such events. As the brigadier entered the office I was working in, my OC introduced me and the other corporal, pointing to me first, and saying, 'This is Corporal Williams and this is Corporal Todd.'

To which the brigadier said, 'No, you're wrong. That is Corporal Todd. I last saw him in Aden wearing a very different uniform.'

It was the adjutant from 15 Signal Regiment. We TOS guys must have left a lasting impression on him!

Due to our travels around the Trucial States and the social events we held at the Scouts Club, we became very friendly with a number of civilian contractors working mainly in the oil industry. One American family lived in a house situated on the road leading out of Dubai towards Jebel Ali. In 2012, when I was with a group of TOS veterans on a visit to what had become the United Arab Emirates, the house was gone. There is now a hotel opposite where it once stood. Its name is the 'Burj Al Arab'; a fantastical, futuristic structure whose existence we could never have imagined during our TOS days.

The loo at Mirfa (flag's up, so it's occupied)

How times have changed! A Texan Family we knew during our service days, had an apartment in the middle of Dubai. We visited them one evening. It was shortly after the Six Day War. Tensions had been running a bit high in various Arab countries. This particular Texan was taking no chances. He had arrived home from work one day, got his shotgun out of its cabinet and sawed about eighteen inches off its barrel. He was very determined about protecting his family. During the evening we were there he was walking around armed with a .38 revolver.

In July '67, I was admitted to the MRS (Medical Reception Station) in Sharjah Camp. I had an abscess at the base of my spine, in a rather delicate area, actually. In true Scouts fashion, a record was requested for me on Forces Radio Sharjah. It was entitled 'Ring of Fire'!

I had to have two operations, but the problem still remained. Finally, it was decided that I must be medevaced back to England.

I was asked by Major Williams, prior to leaving, if I would like to return to the TOS. I certainly did!

I was flown out to Bahrain to await the next medical flight back to England. At the RAF Hospital there, everybody knew I was arriving, so, being a Trucial Oman Scout, I had a bit of a VIP reception.

On the flight to England, there were members of the forces who had been wounded while serving in Aden and Borneo. The medical staff visited all of them, whether they were lying on stretchers or just seated casualties. All was fine until the landing in Cyprus. I think the pilot tried to 'touch down' while the 'plane was still about twenty feet above the runway. It was an extremely hard landing, resulting in everybody being evacuated from the aircraft. Two of the men had to be patched up because their wounds had opened up.

The rest of the journey was uneventful. We landed safely enough at RAF Lyneham. The specially adapted aircraft had side doors, wide enough to allow stretchers to be brought in or out by means of a ramp.

As the doors were being opened, there, riding on the top of the approaching ramp, was a customs officer. He came on board and visited all of us, whether we were in a seat, or strapped to a stretcher, to see if we had anything to declare. Needless to say, some of the answers he received to that question could not be repeated here.

After my operation at the British Military Hospital, Tidworth, I was medically downgraded. I then had a period of leave, prior to being posted to the signals unit nearest the hospital. This was the School of Signals at Blandford. As soon as I got there, I had yet another run in with an RSM. Once again, it was about uniforms. This time it was because I didn't have one!

After a discussion, they realised I would be out of their hair after completion of my medical upgrade. The RSM in his wisdom, because I had been in hospital, decided that I was well-qualified to work in the Medical Centre as an orderly.

About two weeks after that, he came to the Medical Centre looking very sad. He had left the Sergeants' Mess the evening before and had fallen down, lacerating his hands on a cinder path. The doctor examined the RSM then instructed me to clean the wound, ensuring that all the dirt was removed. He knew about the run in between the RSM and myself, and advised me to use a brush on the wound. The doctor had a wicked glint in his eye while he was telling me this. Was it payback time for him?

When I visit Blandford for the Old Comrades Weekend, with veterans of the TOS, I still have a quiet chuckle to myself when I see the Medical Centre.

At long last it was time for my return to the TOS. I discovered that Mike and Bernie Winters were on the flight from Lyneham, along with some other artistes. They were en-route to the Middle East to entertain the military with a series of shows.

During the flight, they kept us entertained. They asked some of us to join them on the wings for a group photo! Considering the political situation at the time, one prank could have gone a bit wrong. At one point, Bernie came out of the toilet and shouted, 'Hi Jack,' to one of the entourage at the other end of the aircraft. Not a good idea on a military flight.

By the time I rejoined the TOS, the British had left Aden, causing the garrison at Sharjah to increase in size. It became known as BTS (British Troops Sharjah). As a result, the TOS had moved from RAF Sharjah to a completely new camp at Al Murgab. The junior NCOs then used the Sergeants' Mess for dining and bar facilities. There was no longer a 'Scouts Club'. Using the sergeants' bar facilities did not suit everybody, but most of us tried to make the best of the shared facilities.

Around this time, the Beatles had a new record album released. It was called, 'Sergeant Pepper's Lonely Hearts Club Band'. This was played quite a few times and we all used to join in the chorus, especially the track entitled, 'When I'm Sixty-Four'. I don't imagine anybody ever thought we would ever be that age. Now all the TOS veterans have surpassed it!

L/Cpl Bob Todd, somewhere in the 'Ulu'.

Forces radio ran a programme for charity. Anybody could phone in and have a record played for a monetary pledge. In the past, the TOS had always managed to donate the most money. Now, however, with the build up of Sharjah Garrison, we were pushed down the list.

Not to be outdone, it was decided that we would go carol singing among the Ex-Pats living in Dubai.

We arranged for the radio station to warn them we were coming and to have their money ready. What we didn't say was that the Pipe-Major would be with us, along with his bagpipes. In Dubai, we entered what was, at that time, considered to be a 'high rise' block of flats; six floors, built around a communal garden.

The residents certainly knew we were there when the Pipe-Major began playing. Residents were shouting down to us from their balconies, asking us to come and join them. I can't remember if we collected any money, but we did spread a lot of happiness that night.

In late 1967, the old way of life began dying, and it was evident that the Trucial States was beginning to develop into a modern land. One of the most prominent improvements was a tarmac road that was being constructed between Abu Dhabi and Buraimi, (Al Ain). The civilian contractors had a mobile camp that kept up with the road as it progressed. The work force's messing was in air-conditioned trailers, similar in most respects to an army Field Mess, but it was unusual to see construction workers drinking out of china cups in theirs! Thanks to the efforts of Corporal 'Tug' Wilson and the generosity of a civilian contractor named Esa Mousa, a Scouts Club was eventually constructed at Al Murgab.

The opening night was a grand affair. Ginger McNamara organised the buffet, a well-kept secret being the centre piece; a suckling pig. How he managed that, in an Arabian country, is anybody's guess.

Whilst visiting Al Magreb in 2012, some of us went out of our way in order to re-visit the Scouts Club. Sadly, it was an empty shell, and not at all how we remember it. Gone is the semi-circular bar, but the canopy above it still remained. Most of the Scouts, at sometime, or other, went fishing at weekends.

A small group of us decided to try night fishing, so in addition to the normal equipment we used, we took a small generator, some lights and a few poles to support them. We booked out of camp and made our way to a location on a deserted beach near Ras Al Khaimah. During the evening, with everything set up, we were fishing away, when we heard gunfire. Looking at one another, we shrugged and agreed that it must be a wedding party. About an hour later, the distinctive sound of someone running in flip flops on hard sand could be heard. The sound increased, and then a figure appeared in the glow of our lights. He ran along the beach, then disappeared into the night. We carried on fishing.

The next morning, a military helicopter came along the coastline and hovered close to our location. We thought no more of it until we returned to camp. We soon learned that there had been an 'incident' near to where we had been fishing. When news of a shooting had reached Al Murgab, our booking-out log had been checked and it was seen that we were in that area. That had been a cause for concern, so a helicopter had been sent to see if we were all right.

British convoy bogged down in subkah

Dave Hobson and I decided that we should build a garden. We knew, of course, that sand is not a very good medium for cultivating plants. Not to be deterred, we collected a few truck loads of manure from the stables and laid out our garden. A daily watering, and we were soon in business, growing tomatoes mainly; along with gourds and an occasional sunflower. The seeds came from the salads on offer in the camp dining room.

Bob Todd and Dave Hobson at work in their garden

One of the other leisure activities available to us was water skiing at Dubai Creek. The RAF supplied us with the most essential piece of equipment; the boat. Indeed, it was almost entirely their show. The problem with water skiing is that, at some point or other, you are going to fall off the skis and end up in the water. It was only when I was actually in the stuff that I remembered I couldn't really swim. Up to that time, splashing about in the shallow end of swimming pools had been the limit of my expertise. We didn't wear life jackets.

Who had heard of, or was even mildly interested in Health and Safety in those days? So, in my case, I decided that while I was in there, struggling to keep afloat and looking for my skis at the same time, I might as well teach myself to swim; which I did, after a fashion.

I also played a bit of hockey. A match was arranged between the TOS and the civilian workers at Das Island, which was an oil terminal south of Abu Dhabi. The transport arrangements were that we were to travel by land to Abu Dhabi and then fly to Das Island, using Gulf Airways. The plane we used was a DC3. Probably war surplus!

At Das, the civilian contractors looked after us. They kept an oar above their bar. It was the type used by professional rowers. We asked how it had got there. Apparently, one of the contractors had brought it out from England. He had arrived at Heathrow, carrying the oar. At check-in, the ground crew insisted that he could not take it on the aircraft. He produced a contract which stated that, in addition to his luggage, he was allowed one piece of sports equipment. He informed the airline staff that he was a rower, and the oar was his one piece of sports equipment.

The SAS, based in the BTS camp at Sharjah, used to spend time in the Scouts Club. One night, after collecting a couple of them, we approached the entrance to Al Murgab. One of the jundee sentries was a bit over-enthusiastic. We stopped the vehicle when he challenged us, but he thrust his rifle, complete with bayonet, right through the side window of the Land Rover. For a moment it looked as though he was going to start shooting. The SAS guys sitting behind us certainly thought so. They told me later that they suspected treachery, and it was only because we were TOS, they hadn't jumped out of the back of the vehicle. They didn't know it, but we were kind of used to that sort of behaviour from Arab sentries.

Amongst all of this, tech tours and repairing generators was the main reason I was in the TOS. Sometimes, emergency repairs had to be carried out in far off places. One such repair entailed me travelling to Mirfa. I was allocated a Land Rover and driver, and left Sharjah. Between Dubai and the Abu Dhabi cross roads there was a stretch of subkha, hard crusted salt flats. If a vehicle left the track, it would sink like a heavy stone placed on a rice pudding. As we were negotiating this terrain, the driver informed me that there was a British convoy up ahead that looked to be in trouble. We parked up to observe it. Sure enough, as soon as they extracted one vehicle from the mire, another one became stuck in it. We approached, to be greeted by the officer in charge, with the words:

'Ah, the Scouts have arrived.'

I don't know what he expected us to do with just a Land Rover. He produced a map and asked how far he was from Al Murgab, at Sharjah. I told him we were only about one hour's travelling time from there. He seemed perplexed by the fact that I didn't have a map. They had left Sharjah twenty four hours earlier, heading for Mirfa, and, having no experience of the terrain, this was as far as they had got.

I stretched out my arm and pointed in the general direction of Mirfa, saying that we were going there as well. It was agreed that we would guide them.

After about an hour had passed, and with more of their vehicles becoming bogged down, I decided I should leave them to it. I still had to carry out the repairs in Mirfa.

We arrived there late in the afternoon, but I completed the repairs and stayed overnight. The following morning, we set off on the return journey to Sharjah. As we approached Abu Dhabi crossroads we saw the convoy, still struggling.

Late one morning, my OC entered the workshop and informed me that I would have to travel to Fujeira as the District Intelligence Officer there was having problems with his generator. This involved a journey through jebel (mountains) to the other side of the Trucial coast, on the Indian Ocean. A helicopter had been booked for my journey, and I was to be ready at the side of the parade ground in half an hour.

I awaited the arrival of a helicopter; and sure enough, one appeared and landed in an immense cloud of dust. I didn't think it was the one I was waiting for, though. It was a Wessex, capable of carrying up to sixteen troops. One of the aircrew walked across to collect me.

After we had stowed my equipment; I was issued with a throat mike and headphones, then asked if I would like to sit in the open doorway. I was fitted with a safety harness and a long strap that was to be secured to the roof of the aircraft. I was still ensuring this was actually secured when we took off. I couldn't hear a thing with those headphones on, so it came as something of a shock when I turned to the open doorway and found we were airborne. I wished I'd had a camera with me on that trip.

With the repairs complete, I was back in Sharjah in time for the evening meal.

During the early summer of 1968 I carried out some courier duties. Wearing civilian clothing, I would collect a briefcase from HQ, before being driven to RAF Sharjah, where I boarded an aircraft. The 'plane in question was an Andover. It could carry up to fifty two passengers, but being the only one travelling on it on these occasions I could pick my own seat. The in-flight service consisted of having access to some soft drinks.

We visited various locations. I was not privy to the contents of the briefcase I carried. Once, when I arrived at Abu Dhabi, I was met at the airstrip and taken to the Political Agency.

When I returned to the aircraft, I was told that it had a fault, so I had to go back to the Political Agency to wait for a spare part to be flown up from Sharjah.

Back at the airstrip I found TWO Andovers waiting for me! An embarrassment of riches for a junior NCO!

It was finally time for me to return to England and to be married. As always, there would be members of the TOS back in the UK, on leave. I ensured that some of them would be at my wedding.

Prior to that taking place, I had an invitation to 'Shady' Harland's house in Gillingham, for a fancy dress party. There was a stipulation that nobody must wear an Arab costume!

My best man was a civilian with the reputation of being a heavy drinker, but he hadn't met the TOS! We put him to bed around nine in the evening at my Stag Party. The next time I was to see him was at my wedding.

On the day before the big event, a few of us somehow ended up in Barnsley. At the end of a long night, we booked into a hotel for what was left of it. I woke up the following morning realising that I was getting married that afternoon! I left a message for the rest of the guys and travelled home. Panic had set in by the time I got there, because nobody knew where I was.

TOS veterans have a common bond, they retain a sense of humour about their ordeals and experiences in those far-off days and maintain a lasting comradeship. When we are together, we are transported back to when we were in our twenties, and remember the question asked on the TOS recruitment poster, 'Are You The Man?' It turned out that we all were, and as such, we are very proud of the role played by the TOS in maintaining law and order in the Trucial States, now known as The United Arab Emirates.

Robert Nelson outside the Sergeants' Mess at Manama in 1969

16

THE JOY OF BEING A TRUCIAL OMAN SCOUT

Robert Nelson Irish Guards

It was a cold night late in 1969 during my guard duties as sergeant of the guard at Windsor Castle that I read a pamphlet about The Trucial Oman Scouts and became hooked on the thought of joining them. The following day I applied to my commanding officer for permission to join the Scouts and, before I knew what was happening, was on an Arabic course at The Army School of Education. A course which I managed to pass by the smallest margin!

In November of 1969 I found myself off to Sharjah. I arrived during Ramadan and the Squadron commander Major Tony Neville allocated me a Land Rover and told the driver not to return until I had visited al of the Scout Squadrons at Al Ayn, Masafi and Ham Ham.

My driver spoke no English and my Arabic was poor, but we got along and the tour of the Squadrons went well.

I was in my element during my time in the Training Squadron and loved every moment of the time I was there. There were four other infantry senior NCOs in the Squadron.

One was Angus McDonald with whom I had a lifetime friendship.

Angus went on to greater things leaving the army and getting a contract with the Arab force in Abu Dhabi, finally ending up within the Sultan's Forces in Oman with the rank of major. Sgt Andy Eikman was another Scot whom I was taking over from and C/Sgt John Bullock of the Army Physical Training Corps and of course, Sgt John Browning of REME.

My first mistake was in my second year when Angus and myself were late back from a party in Dubai. We both overslept the next morning and of course we were whisked away down to Sharjah as it was again Ramadan and we had committed a very serious offence. We both appeared in front of Colonel Chancellor and, boy, did he let fly at us, both being severely reprimanded. You can well imagine the long service and good conduct medal would not be coming to either of us! So I learned a lesson early in my tour, but of course there were many of us who got into little mishaps during our tours. On one occasion, a Squadron officer parked his Land Rover in the middle of a roundabout and went to sleep!

Angus McDonald

My eighteen months passed quickly, much too quickly in fact, and l requested an extension to my time with the scouts and this was granted. In fact, this was the first of several extensions that were granted. We said farewell to Major Tony Nevill and Captain Alan Ball (Cheshire Regiment) and welcomed our new Squadron Commander, Major Graham (Speedy) Hill of the Gloucestershire regiment, and what a character he became as he was not known to attend any function, civilian or otherwise, without falling asleep. Upon completion of his tour, he retired and was manager of the services on the M5 motorway at Exeter but alas, he has now gone to join the other Scout Squadron in the sky.

Our most famed officer would, l think, be Major Ken Wilson, ex Royal Scots. He joined the TOS in 1957 and remained with them until they were transformed into the UDF. Even after all these years he spoke no Arabic at all and it was down to the officers to learn to speak English.

Major Wilson commanded 'X' Squadron who were all Dhofari Arabs and really were a law unto themselves.

My last recollection of this Squadron was when Major Wilson called in on us when we were in our little sergeants' mess at Manama and requested our help. Rebellious factions had infiltrated 'X' Squadron and were causing severe unrest. Angus McDonald, Les Colly and myself accompanied the major back to his Squadron, and as a result we put a good many of the Squadron onto whatever three-ton vehicles were available and took them all to the jail in Dubai. They accepted this and we didn't have a moment's trouble in getting them there. Needless to say, they all spent a considerable time in jail and it was only later, during my service with The Sultan's Armed Forces in Oman, that l learned that the Sultan had declared them to be his prisoners. This resulted in most of them being sent to Muscat and, once there, having sworn allegiance to the Sultan, they were all enlisted into The Firqa Squadron, which to us would be like a Territorial Army. So you can imagine my surprise when l joined the Sultan's Armed Forces in 1974 and met the Firqa Squadron, l found that I was reunited with most of Major Wilson's old 'X' Squadron. My final force commander was Colonel Roy Watson of the Queen's Regiment. He enjoyed coming to Manama, and when he did, never failed to visit our Sergeants' Mess.

The Sergeants' Mess

One trip which will remain with me for a very long time was doing the Liwa Patrol, which was one year the Trucial Oman Scouts and the next year, the Abu Dhabi Defence Force. How our guide was able to lead the patrol across those sand dunes was a talent known only to the local Bedouin Arabs. The patrol commander was Captain Miles Stockwell who had command of our Support Squadron and spoke excellent Arabic. The rule was that we should not have any form of contact with Arab women, but on this patrol, when we arrived in one of the camps in the Empty Quarter, we were invited to tea with the Wali (leader, or chief). Two of his wives came into the tent where we were receiving hospitality. They were both carrying small babies. Without any sign of embarrassment, they opened their dresses and fed the babies as though we were not there. I think this came as a great surprise to us all. I was fortunate enough to do another patrol and it was just as enjoyable as the first for all of us. Captain Miles has to be congratulated on the way the whole patrol was conducted.

Captain Ali Sultana al Kaabi

During my time at Manama, l was fortunate to have two very efficient local Arab officers Captain Ali Sultan and Lt Abdullah Mohammad whom l was able to meet again when we visited the Emirates on our Reunion Tour in 2012. Both have had wonderful careers as Ali had finished as a brigadier and Abdullah went one better, he had finished as a Major General. During my Arabic course at Beaconsfield, Abdullah came over to improve his spoken English and later having him as the recruit officer was a terrific help to me in improving my own Arabic. He was a tower of strength to me in my role as an instructor.

Captain Keith Steel- 'waylaid in a wadi'

There is another amusing story about our commander Col Roy Watson. On his many travels he did not seem to be able to pass Manama without first calling into our small Sergeants' Mess always with our Squadron commander Major Speedy Hill. The trouble was he did not like to leave too quickly and some of his visits could last for two and even three hours! He had a truly lovely lady wife who also visited Manama on several occasions and really enjoyed the company of Angus McDonald and myself. The signals lads would know Mrs. Watson had the call sign COMTESSA and Colonel Watson had SUNRAY. On those occasions that the colonel visited us on his own, it was quite normal that signals for him would be delivered to our mess. All signals to SUNRAY bore the priority prefix.

TOS on patrol in the Liwa

On one occasion, the message was received in our mess from COMTESSA asking for Sunray's location. Colonel Watson replied that he had been called into the small state of Ajman to visit Sheik Rashid. There was an immediate reply to his signal, addressed to Nelson and McDonald, it requested that we please send Sunray back to Sharjah because l know he is still in your mess in Manama.

Wonderful times but we all knew the importance of the work we were doing and this was never lacking. All good times do come to an end, and so it was that, in 1971, the Dubai Defence Force was formed. It was the end of the Trucial Oman Scouts as we knew them, as a completely different defence plan was put in place.

Manama Training Squadron Premier Division football team

I remained with this new force for a further two plus years but somehow it was just not the same as being a Scout. The wearing of berets was introduced and the Scout shemagh as we knew it disappeared. I opted to return to the United Kingdom as I had been invited to join The Sultan's Armed Forces in Oman through my friendship with them, as before mentioned. Angus McDonald, was now commanding a Squadron of Police, Oman Gendarmerie.

After almost four years with the scouts, I came back home, and within a short time found myself on secondment in Oman, where I stayed for five years until my regular release was due.

The years spent with the Scouts will last with me for ever and all has not been forgotten either by us or our friends in the Emirates. What a truly wonderful surprise it was in Feb 2012 to be invited back as guests of the Emirates Government for ten days to enable us to re-live our time there, see how the defence of the Emirates had grown and how the infrastructure of the country had moved into the present times. Of course there was very little comparison to our time. They now have a six-lane motorway as opposed to the sand tracks that led everywhere in our time. However, on our visit to the training Squadron at Manama, we discovered that the original sergeants mess had been allowed to remain just as we remembered it. I was able to look at my old room with the steel bed and the old air conditioners. This is where familiarity ended, because the rest of the camp was in keeping with the modern world. There were beautiful, modern buildings everywhere. It was an amazing experience

We visited all the old Squadron camps some of which are not now used, but allowed to remain as they were. Our mode of travel was two new air-conditioned coaches, stretch Mercedes cars for our senior guests with a fully-equipped ambulance, doctor and two nurses available to us. Absolutely nothing was too much trouble for our hosts, the food was nothing short of exceptional. Everywhere we went and the presents we received, left us all feeling very humble. To think it was all at the expense of the Emirates Government took our breath away.

The local Shaoo tribe came down from the hills and entertained us with their sword dancing which is something I would not recommend anyone to try as it's not for the faint hearted. They presented us all with a small axe each with a few extra to be brought home for some that did make the trip. l was given the task of carrying these axes home by Col Tim Courtney and it was a sight to behold to see me walk through the customs at Heathrow with the axes in clear view. However, nothing was said so, mission accomplished. To see sixty ex-Scouts return to the Emirates says a great deal for the affection we had for our hosts and it was plain to see they had a very high regard for us. l know l speak for all ex-Scouts when l say how wonderful it was to have been part of such a small, but very professional army. Our time with the Scouts will remain with us always.

Once a Trucial Oman Scout, always a Trucial Oman Scout.

2012: Scouts return to the UAE., conveyed in Mercedes coaches and limos
And with an ambulance on standby!

17

THE VIEW FROM THE AIR

Alan England RAF navigator

Upon being presented with my navigator's brevet on graduation in 1966 at RAF Stradishall I felt I had really arrived in the RAF, now I was real 'steely eyed' aircrew. However I soon came down to earth when being informed that I had been posted on Twin Pioneers to RAF Sharjah." Where's that?" I asked myself. Consulting a map I discovered it was part of MEAF [Middle East Air Force] in the Persian Gulf. Then I discovered I was to fly on Scottish Aviation Twin Pioneers! 'What type of aircraft is this?' Research revealed that this was a STOL aircraft used for communications. It had two Alvis Leonidese engines, with slots and flaps operated by chains and sprockets just like a bike [but not as reliable]! Performance was mind boggling, cruising speed was supposed to be 98 Knots; in reality we managed 95 knots. Our maximum range was 600 nm, maximum payload was fourteen passengers. We were also supposed to drop parachutists, not that I was ever subjected to such an arduous task!

They were also equipped with state of the art navigation equipment, drift sight Radio Direction

Finder, which on reaching the Gulf, I found had few stations, of very limited range. We also had the 'Mark One Eyeball' to use with charts which were sparse with information as they dated back to before WW2, not that it made much difference as little had changed since then. I believe the Twin Pioneer was designed for WW2 but was rejected due to its lack of performance.

The Twin Pioneers were employed in moving troops and supplies around the wilderness and on occasions, lending support to the Sultan of Oman. A series of double engine failures caused problems with the Squadron losing two aircraft on the same day. Unsuitable soft and hard landing strips were also causes of failures during landings.

'I did not join the Royal Air Force to be a hero!'

These high speed Gloster Javelin aircraft were stationed at RAF Odiham until the clock was turned back with the arrival of the Twin Pioneer. My crew conversion course, commenced in the middle of winter. Our crew hut was a WW2 prefab, with a coke fire to keep us warm, providing we were not killed by the fumes! No doubt this was all part of making us feel at home with our 'high performance vintage aircraft'.

RAF Gloster Javelin fighters

We were teamed up with our pilots and mine was WO 'Bimbo' Ward. The first time I flew with him I thought, God, he is so overweight he is bound to have a heart attack! I am pleased to say he didn't and proceeded to lose a considerable amount of weight during our tour together.

Training consisted of theory, low level flying at 'low speed' [in fact it was not unusual to be passed by the odd car as we flew over the roads of Hampshire]. We flew so low we even had to gain height to clear the electricity pylons. We also did STOL take offs and landings. I still remember during one sortie, Bimbo, my pilot, wished to visit the loo, which was a bit inconvenient with only one pilot! However, the problem was overcome when he selected one of our STOL landing fields and did a low level beat up to chase the sheep down to one end of the field. As to be expected the sheep were not amused to have their grazing disturbed by this strange machine. We landed, Bimbo got out, went behind the bushes and on completion of his vital task re-boarded the aircraft with a relieved expression on his face! We then took off, much to the pleasure of the disturbed sheep and completed our sortie.

Our three months' conversion course had stretched into six months due to the bad winter of 1966. It was now February 1967, one of the mildest winters the UK had experienced in years!

Next stop, RAF Lyneham then onwards to RAF Muharraq, Bahrain, in the Arabian Gulf, or if you are from Iran, the Persian Gulf.

Having left a warm UK in February it was a great surprise stepping off our "Crab Air" [Royal Air Force Transport Command] VC10 aircraft at Muharraq, Bahrain, to find it was colder than the UK!

At Muharraq we were introduced to our Squadron Leader CO of 152 (Hyderabad) Squadron and OC of A flight, who flew the glamorous high-speed Percival Pembroke aircraft.

We of B flight, with our Flight Lieutenant CO, were based at the sharp end at Sharjah and flew in the illustrious Twin Pioneer aircraft.

A Gulf Air VC10

More avid readers may be interested in the fact that No 152[Hyderabad] Squadron was formed in 1918 as a night fighter Squadron flying Sopwith Camels and was disbanded at the end of the war. It reformed in 1938 as a fighter Squadron with the Gloster Gladiator, soon to be replaced with the Spitfire. The Squadron saw service in the Battle of Britain, Malta and Burma before disbandment. The name 'Hyderabad', together with a Dastard (Ruler's head dress) as the Squadron badge, was in recognition of the donation of Spitfires to the RAF by the Nizam of Hyderabad.

Arrival at RAF Sharjah, with a Wing Commander CO, was like stepping back in time. The control tower was in a 'Beau Geste' type fort.

All six of us new boys on B flight, three pilots and three navigators, then had a formal presentation by Colonel Freddie de Butts, the CO of the Trucial Oman Scouts [TOS] of our shemagh and aghul (the black cord that held it in place on the head)

Raf Muharraq, Bahrein 1967

Muharraq International Airport, Bahrein- today

Our major role was working with the TOS, doing communication, exercises, casevac and supply. One of our less glamorous tasks was flying to Ras al Khaimah for the fruit and vegetable run.

We would load up the aircraft, fumigate it, then board it ten minutes later to find the cockpit temperature over 140 F and full of dead flies! Do not remember that in the advertisement about becoming 'steely eyed aircrew'!

Some of the airstrips that we used included: Jebel Akhdar, Muscat, 6000 feet up.

The runway was very short, and had a sheer drop at one end and a mountain at the other. The remains of a Venom aircraft lay at one end, shot down by insurgents. Fortunately they had been sorted out by the Trucial Oman Scouts and the SAS.

RAF Salalah, Muscat was still the scene of a raging insurgency. During one of my visits I was able to have a flight in a Sultan of Oman Air Force Short Skyvan, flown by one of our ex-Squadron pilots. We also flew to RAF Masirah, where great pleasure was gained in showing visiting 'Crab Air' aircrew to the toilet when requesting directions to the TV room.

We had no TV in the Gulf. I was also fortunate to view the turtles laying their eggs on the island, one of the few spots this event occurs worldwide.

RAF Masirah

When on visits to the desert airfield strip at Seeb outside the capital of Muscat, you had to ensure that you were well equipped, for the town gates were locked at sunset and you were then only able to walk about the town with a lantern; how different it is today as the hub of a vibrant tourist industry.

Burami Oasis with its Beau Geste fort was the scene of confrontation with Saudi Arabia in 1955 until it was sorted out by the TOS.

Liwa Hollows was in the middle of nowhere, with the strip carved into dunes 300 feet high. On one occasion we had to abort the flight when our primary navigation aid, The Mark 1 Eyeball failed due to poor visibility!

During the course of my tour I indulged in sailing. I was able to take sailing teams to Bahrain and

Abu Dhabi; we were air lifted out from the sailing club by helicopter. In those days it was easy to arrange air transport. However, sailing came to an abrupt end during the Arab/ Israeli Six Day War when the sailing compound was burnt down together with our two catamarans. Some Palestinians saw visiting RAF Hunter aircraft taking off for the gunnery range and they thought they were en route for Israel! Would you believe the next day we had some Palestinians visit the sick bay with burns admitting how they got burnt! The local sheikh dealt with the problem by giving free transport by boat to volunteers to join the war! Problem solved.

I was also able to take up riding, as the TOS felt it was part of their tradition to have horses not just any old horses, but beautiful Arab horses, which needed exercising. So I frequently took to riding on the beach at dawn, with the horse being in charge rather than the rider!

The biggest event to affect me was when the CO volunteered me to set up and run a desert survival school! Unfortunately I was unable to come up with any good reasons to get out of this mission. I was sent to RAF El Adem, Libya for training, this was to take nearly a month, as I had to go by "Crab Air" VC10 via Muharraq to Cyprus, which was easy enough. The problem was Cyprus to El Adem. My first attempt in a Canberra aircraft ended at the end of the runway when the aircraft aborted the take off!

Eventually I made it by a Hastings, via Malta [cannot escape the place], where I took the liberty of having a few days R&R.

If you were unfortunate enough to be stationed at RAF El Adem you used to refer to it as "the a*** hole of the world" but twenty miles up it as that was the distance of El Adem from the sea!

DH Comet at RAF Sharjah

After the course, which I have to admit had not enhanced my knowledge, I returned to Sharjah, borrowed a Land rover from the desert survival team, put on my 'Lawrence of Arabia' gear and set out into the desert to find a suitable site to run the survival school. Fortunately, I got slightly lost and ended up in an encampment run by a Scotsman drilling for water. So, after a swim in the pool, a curry supper and leaving him with a bottle of whisky, I departed knowing that I had found my ideal site. Thereafter, I was able to run a few survival courses in great safety. While the 'victims' survived in their tents with temperatures of 130 F and even had the odd Bedouin visit, requesting water from their rations, yours truly enjoyed a swim, a curry supper and nights in an air-conditioned tent, all for the price of a bottle of whisky. I also received an AOC commendation!

Short Skyvan flying above Salalah. Unfortunately the insurgents were still active and the odd mortar was lobbed at the air strip

I also have memories of my Honda motor bike running out of petrol en route to Dubai, fortunately the local AA were very good, the first lorry stopped, put the bike in the back and dropped me off at the nearest petrol station, no charge. The Trucial Oman Scouts certainly knew how to entertain with their TOS Ball, which had a 'surplus of women', as they had, at great cost, been flown in from all over the Gulf. Yours truly arrived at the mess at 2000 hours to be greeted by a piper and departed the next day at 0800; I can say it was the best function I had ever attended.

Canberra PR9 bomber

During our tour we were given the choice of a free flight to UK for R&R or two weeks in Kenya, which included a weeks safari and a week in the 5* Norfolk Hotel, Nairobi, all inclusive, with flight, for £35! -yes, you guessed correctly, this was the option I took a RAF Argosy flight to Aden a few weeks before British forces finally pulled out of Aden forever! Then by East African Airways Comet aircraft.

Armstrong Whitworth Argosy,
also known as the 'Clockwork Mouse' or the 'Whistling Wheelbarrow'

Unfortunately the good life came to an end in September and we became part of the real RAF, with the closure of Aden.

Argosy aircraft were then based at Sharjah and we had a Group Captain CO. Finally, on the 15 November 1967 the illustrious 152 Hyderabad Squadron was disbanded at RAF Muharraq. Today Dubai, Abu Dhabi, Muscat have all developed and become tourist destinations, a far cry from the sort of places they had been when I was posted to Sharjah. Little did I realise then that it was to be the end of an era, one that I have been fortunate and privileged to participate in.

Leaving 152 Squadron and the Trucial Oman in a warm November 1967 I was posted to 267 Squadron at RAF Benson to fly in an Argosy.

A busy RAF Sharjah, with an Anson, Beverley and Twin Pioneer lined up

18

THE TOS BOYS' SCHOOL-MY STORY

Dr Saif al Bedwawi PhD

In 1951 the Trucial Oman Levies were established in Sharjah to serve the seven Sheikhdoms. The idea was to recruit locals to serve in the force in the long run. They were, however, mostly illiterate and had no understanding of the modern machinery, communication systems, etc used by the TOL. That brought about the establishment of the Boys' School in Manama, later moved to Sharjah. Here is the story of my life in the Boys' School which I joined in 1966.

In 1954, Eric Johnson, Deputy Force Commander of the TOL, collected a number of local boys together and opened a small school in Manama.

Initially, Sergeant Omar Saeed, from Aden, was the only teacher. Besides learning to read and write basic Arabic, mathematics were taught, along with some military training, such as drill. In an inspired move, the school concentrated in teaching army signalling techniques, including sending and receiving Morse code; the system the TOL, and later, the TOS, used to communicate with their squadrons and outstations.

Some of the boys had a natural ability with Morse, and when they emerged from training, British Signallers found that they could hardly compete with them when it came to speed and accuracy.

Captain Page teaching al fresco

Esa Mousa, Nair in the middle and a visitor

Admission to the school depended on the health of the student; priority being given to those boys
who already had a member of his family serving in the TOL/S. In addition to that, loyalties being all-important, the question that was put to each applicant was, 'Who is your Sheikh?' By 1959, the school had developed into a small, but professional institution with several teachers and a British Head Master from the Royal Army Education Corps.

The first of these was Captain Clem Page. In 1967, the school was moved to Murgab, the new TOS camp in al Heirah. The number of pupils had multiplied, as had the teachers.

Omar Nisnas, a Palestinian from Jordan, became a very influential figure in the school. He brought in good teachers from Jordan, such as Allan, Mohammed Khamis, and Jawdat.

In 1965 I went to a local school in Masfut to study the Quran and the Arabic alphabet. My older brother was already in the Boys' School and he asked me to go along with him to Sharjah, and enlist.

I saw Ali bin Aboud, who was in charge of training the boys in military drill and looked after their barracks. He introduced me to a man called Nair, an Indian in charge of recruitment. He took a photograph of me and issued me with a number which was 4933. That is the military number which I still use to this day in order to help me remember my computer passwords!

On Parade in 1971 at Murgab

It was nice to wear a military uniform; it made me feel that I was a big man. I was provided with various articles of clothing, including sandals, shemagh, khunja and boys' dress. I managed to wear the unfamiliar outfit the next day, putting it on with some help from my brother. As far as the classes were concerned, I had been given ability tests and told that I would go to the second class. I was not sure if that meant good or bad, until I received the books. They were not so difficult, but I had to study hard to understand the maths and English.

The subjects we took were as follows: Arabic language, English language, religious studies, social studies, Maths, and sciences. Arab students found it difficult to pronounce the English letter "P" because there is no such letter in Arabic.

Captain Derek Dykins, the headmaster from 1966-1971, insisted that we must pronounce it correctly.

Accordingly, the English teacher used to cut a piece of paper and put in his hand, then ask us all to purse our lips and say "P" as loudly as possible. If we did not blow the paper from his hand our pronunciation was not accurate enough! Me and my classmate used to spend hours cutting pieces of paper and shout "P. P ", at them, but they did not fly!

After graduating from the Boys' School in 1971, my classmates and I were asked to decide if we would like to go to the Trade School in Dubai, or to the Depot in Manama. Well, the Depot was rather horrifying to me at that time because they used to drill the recruits all the way from Manama to Sharjah and live in the desert for nights on end! I applied to study commerce in the Trade School and continue to live in Murgab Camp. My decision was not accepted by my family because they wanted me to work as a soldier and make some money. Well, I'm afraid I did not obey them, and I was accepted by the Trade School.

Captain Derek Dykins

We used to take a Bedford from Murgab to Dubai every day and come back in it at around two in the afternoon. The headmaster was British. His name was Mr Taylor, and he came from the Development Office, which was in the care of Her Majesty's Political Agent. I managed to reach the top of my class and by 1975 had won a scholarship to Beirut to study commerce.

Unfortunately, Lebanon had witnessed a civil war, jeopardising my scholarship for a while. I was sent to work in the Ministry of Defence because it was now in charge of the Union Defence Force.

In 1976, I was called on by the Ministry of Education to go to California. I had no idea where that was! I asked my family's permission, but they wanted me to get married.

I told them that I had no money and I was still a boy with less than 500 Dirhams monthly salary.

After spending ten years in California doing my graduate studies and Masters' degree, I went back to the Ministry of Defence. I told them that I wanted to go for further studies in the United Kingdom in order to gain a Doctorate. My request was not well received by the assistant secretary. When I pressed him about it, he said that my files were lost due to the amalgamation of the UDF with other armed forces. That was good news as far as I was concerned, because it eventually allowed me to get what I wanted and continue studying for my Doctorate and gain a PhD from Durham University.

Boys' School Cmp at Fujairah 1970

Eventually, my wife and our four children all went to Durham, after I passed my viva. My research for my PhD relied heavily on interviewing Britons who had worked and served in the Gulf States. They included such important personalities as: Sir James Craig, a former Political Agent in Dubai, Michael Tait, the former UK Ambassador to the UAE, some well-known bankers and former employees of Grey Mackenzie, such as George Chapman. I also interviewed many former British officers who had served in the Gulf States, including Colonel De Butts and the last British commander of the TOS.

Impact of TOS Boys' School on UAE Military culture:

The legacy left by the Trucial Oman Scouts Boys' School survives today in the Emirates. Firstly, most of the commanders of the UAE forces were educated and received their initial military training at the Boys' School. Secondly: the original curriculum introduced at the Boys'

School is still practiced in the new military schools; these include methods of learning signals techniques, military music, map reading, and drill. Many graduates of the Boys' School went on to achieve high rank in the UDF and continually prove that they remain totally loyal to fine military values, discipline and culture that was established so long ago.

  Even though I left Boys' School many years ago, my classmates of that time are still the best friends I have. We occasionally meet to talk about our teachers and tell jokes about our old salary of 90 rupees. I am proud to say that studying in the TOS Boys' School enhanced my ambition to become their first graduate to hold a PhD from a competitive university. That encouraged me to work in the Zayed Military College, where I was in charge of academic studies until I retired with the rank of lieutenant colonel in the year 2000.

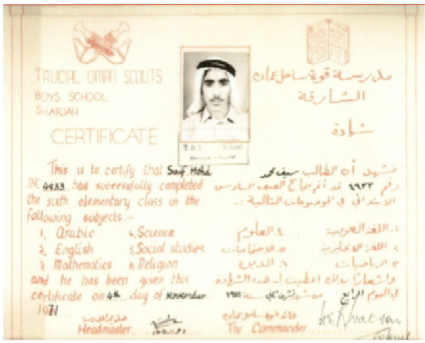

My certificate in 1971

TOS Medical Reception Station, Sharjah 1967

19

REMINISCENCES OF A RADIOGRAPHER

Philip Yorke RAMC

I was an unmarried soldier in 1966, and known for my willingness to go anywhere at the drop of the proverbial hat. While stationed at the Royal Herbert Hospital, Woolwich, I was asked by the OC of the X-ray School if I would volunteer for a secondment to the Trucial Oman Scouts. After enquiring who they were, I quickly agreed to go.

Time passed by and I was posted to the Cambridge Military Hospital in Aldershot without having heard anything further.

Around about October I was asked by a colleague if I would make up a foursome, since he wanted to take a young lady he was interested in, out for a meal. She had refused to go with him unless she had a friend with her. Being footloose and fancy free, I agreed to his request. It was then that Cupid's arrow struck, because after meeting the girl I was partnered with, I started courting her, to use an old fashioned phrase.

Just before Christmas of that year, a pre-posting order came through, warning me that I was going to the Trucial Oman Scouts in April 1967. Having already talked about committing matrimony, I decided to propose in a cattle class carriage coming back from a visit to a show in

London.

I was accepted. I must admit that we also had our eyes on the fact that by getting married before my posting, we would gain the benefits of unaccompanied marriage allowance, extra points for quarters, etc.

So in March of '67 the knot was tied in St Giles' Cathedral, Edinburgh. After learning of our engagement, many unworthy minds were mentally counting up to nine on their fingers because of the speed in which we had tied the knot. A month later I was in Sharjah, but not until after a series of dramatic events.

I was due to travel from Aldershot to Gatwick on a Sunday morning. The duty driver was late collecting me, so I missed the train. I ordered him to continue to Redhill, in the hope that I might be able to catch the next connection - but no joy. I eventually arrived at Gatwick to be told that the plane had just taken off. Its departure had been held back for me, but it could wait no longer. The RTO wanted to know why I was late, but upon checking my movement order we found that the times given were for the previous day! So I escaped being put on a charge.

I spent the night in a transit holding in North London before being successfully transported to Sharjah the next day.

I was met by Harry Davies, who I had first encountered in Hong Kong in 1958. I was shocked to be told by my new CO at the MRS (Medical Reception Station) that I was not actually going to be with the TOS, but with British Troops Sharjah (BTS) when they arrived later in the year. I was not a happy bunny at this news and protested that I had been asked to volunteer for this posting and I certainly would not have done so if I had known I was being posted to the BTS. Suffice to say, he agreed with me and started to pull various strings.

A few days later I was issued with my shemagh and aghul.

My first memory of meeting the dental officer is that he was sat behind his desk doing some embroidery! My last is that, his horse having died under him while he was riding it back from Al Hira, he had to carry the saddle and other tack all the way to the camp, on foot, in the scorching heat. He was not best pleased.

About a week after my arrival the MRS, Company Sergeant Major Frank Baker approached me to ask what my religious leanings were. I thought this odd, because if he wanted to know, he could have looked at my Q & R card in the office, or else asked to see my ID. His initial question developed into a situation where he would not tell me his unless I told him mine, and I would not tell him mine until he told me his! In the end, he said,

'You're not Jewish, are you?' To which I replied,

'No.'

He said, 'Thank heavens for that!'

When I asked why, he replied, 'Well, you look a bit Jewish, and the Arab ambulance drivers think you are.'

'What's it got to do with them?'

'Well, I've heard a rumour that they're planning to kill you!'

A few days later the Arab - Israeli war broke out!

While this short war was going on, Nasser's rabble rousers occupied themselves by burning down our boat club in Sharjah and destroying some of our yachts. They also went around smashing and looting British and French shops and cars in Dubai. Our jundies (private soldiers) were called out to help the local police. They were led by our Arab officers and NCOs, but directed by the British, who were out of sight, but kept in touch by radio.

*Obituary for the founding father of modern Dubai,
Sheikh Rashid bin Said al Maktoum*

When the rabble rousers were rounded up, the first group were told by Sheikh Rashid that if they wanted to support Nasser, that was quite all right by him and he shipped them off to Egypt by plane on a one-way ticket. By the time the next lot were tried, Nasser had called it quits, but Rashid put them on a dhow and towed them about two miles out to sea, over the harbour bar where there was a heavy swell, and left them there for two days without food or water. Their only company was a patrol boat chugging back and forth - not to prevent them escaping, because Rashid in his wisdom realised that none, if any, could swim - but to ensure that no one came from the shore to help them to either escape or bring them supplies. Two days later they were brought back to shore. Seasick and unsteady they staggered onto dry land.

It was about six months later that the first of those who were sent to Cairo started to return. Many of the shops and businesses in Dubai had Nasser's photograph hanging in their premises in those days. Sheikh Rashid sent his men, unannounced, into these and demanded a levy to be paid to cover the cost of the air transportation of those sent north. It was amazing how quickly those pictures of Nasser disappeared to be replaced by those of the Sheikh!

At the same time, there was great consternation among the locals who thought we were sending help to Israel in the form of a tank.

Our Armoured Support Squadron, the Queen's Dragoon Guards were having an exercise in which they were using what I think was an old Centurion tank. When it went rumbling out of camp, the rumour went round the town that we were sending it to Egypt to help Israel!

Obviously, they had no sense of the logistics that would be involved to achieve that feat.

Calm was restored when it returned later that day!

Unfortunately, being the only radiographer in camp, I never had the opportunity to visit the units up country. This had been the situation for my predecessor. He only left the camp three times in the two years he was there, and two of those occasions were when we were handing/taking over. He had developed the habit of watching the films in the open air cinema by sitting on the roof of his billet and viewing them through his Yashica binoculars. He was a Scot with a very broad Glaswegian accent. So broad in fact, that even fellow Glaswegians had difficulty in understanding him. The story goes that when the Admiral Middle East Land Forces visited Sharjah, he called in on the X-ray Dept where he was met by the Scotsman. When the admiral asked him if there was anything in his department that he could do with, the reply he gave, freely translated, was that he could do with an image intensifier so that he could undertake barium meal tests and give enemas, amongst other things. The Admiral, obviously a clued-up chap, replied that Jock did not have a big enough workload to justify one, and if he did have an image intensifier, he would also require a radiologist. He then asked if there was anything else he would like. The answer this time, again being freely translated, was that he would like to have done the colloquial Arabic course before coming out, so that he could talk to the jundies (private soldiers) in their own language, and not through an interpreter. To which the Admiral replied that perhaps Jock should have taken a colloquial English course first, so that everyone could understand him! Strangely enough, he was fluent in about five languages, and spoke without a trace of accent.

I found a wing commander with his hand wrapped in bandages, waiting for me in the MRS. Apparently, he had been teaching some new recruits how to water-ski and showing them 'what not to do, when he was struck by the propeller of the towing boat. I removed the mass of bandages and he saw the cut, he passed out. When the RAF medic and I bought him round, he took another look and fainted again. This happened a third time, so I decided that while he was 'out' I would take the images required. As it happened, he was lucky in that he hadn't suffered any damage to his hand, other than it requiring some stitches.

Another patient, an illegal immigrant, was sent in from the state prison so that his neck could be X–rayed. It was severely swollen and he had difficulty in breathing. The X-ray revealed a cancerous growth that was causing the oedema and breathing problem. Being an illegal, the Al Maktoum Hospital in Dubai would not accept him for treatment so he was given a morphine cocktail by us in the form of a plasticine-like ball. From this, he could pick off a piece to suck to help alleviate any pain. He was returned to prison and then sent back to Baluchistan, presumably to die.

Yet another patient, not mine, was admitted. When the ward staff went to check on him, they found him lying in a pool of blood. He had decided that when he was circumcised, the job had not been done well enough for his liking, so he'd decided to improve on it. To do this, he dismantled a razor and started to operate on himself. In doing so, he had cut a small artery. He would have bled to death, but for the prompt action of the nursing orderlies. In a similar vein, if you will excuse the pun, two young boys were brought in. They were suffering from badly-botched circumcisions. Instead of using a knife to circumcise them, a set of bone nibblers had been used. The idea being that, if the foreskin was pulled far enough over the glans penis and sufficient pressure was applied, the supply of blood would be stopped and the skin would eventually come away on its own. A good idea in theory, but not if the instrument is not sterile, which was the case in this instance. This amateur op resulted in a festering mass, so the unfortunate boys were sent to us for treatment.

A Queen's Dragoon Guards armoured vehicle ran out of juice in the desert. Having refilled. The driver poured a little petrol into the carburettor to help start the engine. With the combination of the heat of the engine and the surrounding air, the petrol vaporized. Then a few drops fell onto the engine. A flash of fire and the driver was set alight. Fortunately for him, he was quickly rolled in the sand to put out the flames, but not before he suffered fifty per cent burns to the front of his body, including blisters to his manhood. The medic with the patrol applied Vaseline gauze dressings to his burns in the absence of water.
The driver was casevaced to the UK by the RAF.

At sometime or other, someone had founded a Royal Antediluvian Order of Buffaloes Lodge in Sharjah Camp. Several Trucial Oman Scouts were members of this world-wide, fraternal brotherhood, commonly known as 'The Buffs'. Among the civilian members was Sheikh Khalid bin Mohamed al Qasimi. In a coup, typical of the era, Khalid's uncle had been deposed as Sheikh of Sharjah. Another civilian member, Gerry Wain, was the manager of the Dubai Water Works. Gerry told me that Sheikh Rashid of Dubai regarded the tribesmen as 'his children'. In order to try and restrict their movements from one well to another, he had ordered Gerry to take men and equipment out to the sites and drill down to the water table beyond the depth of the wells. He was to install pumps above ground so that water could be brought to the surface when the wells ran dry. The pumps' fuel tanks were designed in such a manner as to deny the tribesmen access to them. When they ran dry, they were obliged to, as the Sheikh was said to have put it,
'Send a runner to me with a message in a cleft stick and I will send you the fuel.' This helped tie the people to the water pumps, and to him. To further induce settlement, Sheikh Rashid also paid his people one Riyal a day for every child they sent to school. This all helped bring the traditional, nomadic existence to an end – and educated the future generations.
Before the local water supply was properly treated it had an extremely high fluoride content. This caused a very serious health problem called Fluorosis. Quite often, when taking X-rays of a Bedu's torso, I would ask him to take a deep breath and nothing appeared to move. The resulting X-ray would reveal that the man's ribs were like strips of concrete. Excessive amounts of calcium in the skull at an early age meant that, while the brain was expanding, the cranium was not.

The poor child would die in agony. Thanks to Sheikh Rashid and Gerry Wain and others, this severe problem was eradicated.

A typical desert well.

If I achieved anything at all in Sharjah, it was during my three months as Mess Manager. I inherited the equivalent of a two hundred and fifty pounds deficit in the catering fund and handed over a healthy surplus thanks to the Arab cook in the kitchen. It was he who suggested that I went with him to the dockside in order to buy fresh fish straight from the dhows, and to the souk for vegetables etc. He also suggested buying a sack of dried prawns which he could soak overnight when he was preparing a curry. Good man, that chef.

A disappointing piece of news came through. I was told that my secondment was being taken over by the BTS after all. I was not the only one to lose my job. Both the dental technician and the medical store man were being replaced at the same time. So it was back to the UK

My connection with the Trucial Oman Scouts should have ended there, but many years after I left the force, I saw an advertisement in the Royal British Legion magazine, announcing a forthcoming reunion of the TOS Association. After joining the association, I eventually had the honour of becoming its treasurer.

Phillip Yorke, on the right, visits Sheikh Zayed Mosque in 2012

Left to right, standing: Cpl Irvine, L/Cpl Phillips, L/Cpl McCraik, Sgt Steel, Cpl Brelsford, Cpl Rose, Cpl Hadfield, Cpl Lee and Cpl Hewitt Sitting: Sgt Erskine, Sgt Lee, SSM Anderson, Capt Picot, Col L Brooks, Lt Col L V Bageley, Maj E Matson, SQMS Barnett, SQMS Bridges and Sgt Peterson

20

LAST DAYS

Dennis Irvine RAOC

  Duty clerks get the opportunity to read many military manuals. Manual of Military Law, Queen's Regulations and a host of others. The Secondment Manual was the one that interested me most, though. I was drawn to those forces that offered opportunities for adventure, the satisfaction of serving with foreign forces and experiencing their cultures.

  I had never served in the Middle East and I was single at the time. I applied for service in the TOS and got on with life in the British Army Of the Rhine. I heard nothing for some considerable time. It was when I was serving in a Forward Ammunition Depot that a posting order duly arrived, with a move date of December 3rd 1970.

  Having married in 1967, and with a child aged two years, there was a serious decision to be made. I knew that if I opted to have the posting cancelled it would be entirely possible that I would not be considered for another secondment. My wife and I agreed that it was in the best interests of my career to accept, so the wheels were set in motion.

My family returned to Malaysia and I went off to Sharjah via Brize Norton and Bahrain. Upon arrival at Sharjah I was transported to Al Hira Camp. It would be my home until October 1972.

By the time I arrived, the TOS had five Rifle Squadrons, a Support Group with mortars and GPMGs which were deployed across the TOS areas of responsibilities. They rotated on a 6 monthly basis with the exception of 'X' Squadron.

Al Hira Camp also contained the Force Headquarters, Signals and Transport Squadron and a hospital, together with vehicle workshops and a Quartermaster's Store. There was a Boys School for young Arabs and a Mounted Troop. The TOS stores organization which, in real terms was the equivalent of the role usually played by the Ordnance Corps, was headed by a British Major, assisted by a British Captain and an Arab Captain. Their functions were many and varied with responsibility for the provision of arms, vehicles and manifold general items including the maintenance and issue of fuel and fodder. The stores organization also carried out work in connection with movements and shipping. During my time, over thirty per cent of the British contingent in the TOS were Royal Army Ordnance Corps personnel.

At Hira Camp-also known as Murgab

For fairly obvious reasons, one of the most popular men in camp was the Post NCO. He bravely attempted to create a garden in the sand between two accommodation blocks. Little, if anything, grew, so his plan to supply the kitchen with fresh produce came to nothing. He was the only one of us not to realize it was doomed from the outset!

Another NCO acquired a Turtle and constructed a pond for it to live in. The novelty of having it around soon wore off, so it was returned to the sea. Then some of the corporals got hold of a monkey by some means or other.

They built a cage for it, and the mischievous animal became so popular it was allowed to sit at the bar in the Scouts Club and enjoy a drink from his personal ashtray.

The monkey took a dislike to me and chased me out of the club one afternoon. After biting my rear end, it made its way back into the club. Terrified that I might get rabies, I applied liberal amounts of Dettol to my wound and made my way to the Medical Centre. After running amok in one of the accommodation blocks it was taken for a trip on a boat. Sadly enough, while off the coast of Ajman, it jumped overboard, swam to the shore and was never seen again.

On exercise: Capt John Picot, Cpl Robin Daniels RAMC and Dennis Irvine

In 1971, The Trucial Oman Scouts, having maintained the peace in an unsettled region for twenty years, was turned over to Arab control and became the nucleus of the Union Defence Force for the United Arab Emirates, a new and extraordinarily wealthy nation formed out of seven Sheikhdoms. Some TOS men, including me, slipped easily into this new force and 'soldiered on' until our secondment expired.

When I left the Union Defence Force in 1972, I was a sergeant aged 25. Later on, I had a further Secondment, this time to the Royal Brunei Malay Regiment. I then served as a member of the British Army Training and Liaison Staff at Kahawa Camp, just outside Nairobi. I was commissioned and retired from the army as a lieutenant colonel in the year 2002. I feel that I owe it all to my memorable tour with the Trucial Oman Scouts. Like many others who took the opportunity to serve with them, and proved that they were indeed, 'The Man', the experience launched me into a life I dared hardly aspire to at the time.

His Highness Sheikh Zayed bin Sultan al Nahayan, President of the UAE
At the annual rifle meeting in 1976

The Trucial Oman Scouts pass in to history

21

THE LAST HURRAH

Captain Tim Courtenay, 2ic 'A' Squadron, Trucial Oman Scouts 68/70 Reunion Co-ordinator
60th Anniversary Reunion in The United Arab Emirates 2nd-11th March 2012

At the invitation of Lt Gen Hamad Mohammad Thani al Romethi, Chief of Defence Staff of the UAE Armed Forces, 60 Veterans of The Trucial Oman Scouts and Union Defence Force returned for a 10 day trip back to the country in which we once served. The aims were threefold, to visit the sites of our Squadron locations, renew friendships with Arab officers and soldiers with whom we once served, and see some of the sights and sounds of this young, modern and dynamic Nation.

Through the good offices of the senior Contract Officer Maj Gen Andrew Pillar and his successor Brig Geoff Sheldon the ground rules were established and a draft programme and administrative details were produced.

The lead staff officer was Major Richard Kettle a former Royal Marine, and his dedicated hard work and patience, including arranging flights for the party as well as ground recces of locations, ensured that once on the ground our programme went without a hitch. We travelled in two air conditioned coaches accompanied by two Mercedes 350S Class AMG Protocol staff cars. These gave us the flexibility to divert presentation teams to the seven Rulers as and when they were able to see us.

Gifts were considered as a high priority and Lt Col David Sievwright and Hugh Nicklin produced special TOS Coupelles and some photograph albums covering the period 1951 to 1975. In addition, David Shepherd, the artist of Jahili Fort authorised a special reproduction of 10 only from a print that had been signed by Sheikh Zayed, Sheikh Kalifa bin Zayed, Sheikh Tachnoon and Sheikh Faisal Sultan back in 1969.

The gifts were given to our hosts as we crisscrossed the country and were very well received.

All members of the visiting group contributed £145 each to this project. Suffice it to say we were showered with gifts from medallions to briefcases, to watches and statuettes, for which we are most grateful and will provide lasting memories for us, and our families of a visit of a lifetime. The principal group gifts are being held centrally and will eventually be housed in the Trucial Oman Scouts Archive at the School of Islamic and Arabic Studies in Exeter University

Veterans travelled from as far afield as Canada, Australia, Germany and Cyprus as well, of course, England, Wales, Northern Ireland and Scotland, the home of our President, Lt Gen Sir John MacMillan KCB, CBE, DL who played his part to the full as our "Front Man" attending to the Rulers, making speeches and presenting gifts as our caravan progressed. HQ UAE Armed Forces provided us with a splendid team of Escorts led by Lt Col Pilot Saeed Abdullah al Shihail, Dr Lt Col Saeed Hamed al Kalabani, Dr Capt Manie Hamad al Shimaili and Lieutenant Mohammed Mubarack al Awani and Mr Abdullah Allah Naseeb al Kitibi from the Protocol Office. They along with a team of medical staff and drivers were our caring and guiding force to whom we are most grateful.

Our "Roller Coaster Magic Carpet" finally landed back at Heathrow on the 11th March. The "Biblical" land we once knew has exploded onto a modem, dynamic young Nation with a firm place on the World Stage. We, as small grains of sand in the scheme of things, are very proud and humbled to think that in our days of training "Jundees" we were actually training the future leaders of a great new nation, "The United Arab Emirates".

Trucial Oman Scouts and Union Defence Force Veterans Reunion

Printed in Great Britain
by Amazon